Living Now

———•———

Barbara Phillips

Living Now

———•———

Joel S. Goldsmith

EDITED BY LORRAINE SINKLER

THE CITADEL PRESS · SECAUCUS, N.J.

Except the Lord build the house, they
labour in vain that build it.

—PSALM 127

Illumination dissolves all material ties and binds men together with the golden chains of spiritual understanding; it acknowledges only the leadership of the Christ; it has no ritual but the divine, impersonal, universal Love, no other worship than the inner Flame that is ever lit at the shrine of Spirit. This union is the free state of spiritual brotherhood. The only restraint is the discipline of Soul; therefore, we know liberty without license; we are a united universe without physical limits, a divine service to God without ceremony or creed. The illumined walk without fear—by Grace.

—*The Infinite Way*

Contents

———•———

Living Now

O N E

Living Now

Above all things, the message of The Infinite Way emphasizes the dignity and infinite nature of individual man, revealing that we are always in control of our own destiny because of our oneness with our Source. To accept this spiritual status means also to accept the responsibility to let the divine Spirit live our life

EDITOR'S NOTE: The material in *Living Now* first appeared in 1963 in the form of letters sent to students of The Infinite Way throughout the world in the hope that they would aid in the revelation and unfoldment of the transcendental Consciousness through a deeper understanding of Scripture and the practice of meditation.

The italicized portions are spontaneous meditations that came to the author during periods of uplifted consciousness and are not in any sense intended to be used as affirmations, denials, or formulas. They have been inserted in this book from time to time to serve as examples of the free flowing of the Spirit. As the reader practices the Presence, he, too, in his exalted moments, will receive ever new and fresh inspiration as the outpouring of the Spirit.

and not permit it to be lived for us by the universal beliefs of this world—economic, medical, or theological—but rather to live a life governed by the truth.

The thesis laid down by the Master was: "Ye shall know the truth, and the truth shall make you free" [1]; and inasmuch as we accept the guidance of Christ Jesus, who laid out the Way for us, the truth that we must know is the truth that he has given us:

> "I and my Father are one.[2] . . . Son, thou art ever with me, and all that I have is thine.[3] . . . I am the way"—not the conditions outside, and not the people outside. "I am the way, the truth, and the life.[4] . . . I am come that they might have life, and that they might have it more abundantly" [5]—healthfully, joyously, freely, intelligently. "I will never leave thee, nor forsake thee.[6] . . . I am with you alway, even unto the end of the world." [7]

The truth that we must know is that from the beginning of time God has planted in the midst of us that which is to be our saviour, our power, and our dominion, dominion over everything in the earth and above the earth and beneath the earth. Although we have gradually let this dominion slip away from us, by knowing the truth we can recapture it and once again live freely, sharing that life of abundance and joy with all who are receptive and responsive to it.

Every Day Is a Day of Decision

In the first few days of a New Year, it is customary to greet one another many, many times with "Happy New Year," but in the

[1] John 8:32.
[2] John 10:30.
[3] Luke 15:31.
[4] John 14:6.
[5] John 10:10.
[6] Hebrews 13:5.
[7] Matthew 28:20.

very act of saying and hearing "Happy New Year" so often, let us be ever mindful that a happy New Year cannot come to us. There is nothing in the atmosphere that can act upon us to give us a happy New Year, and, unless we permit it, there is nothing in the atmosphere to give us an unhappy one.

Who is there who is concerned whether we have a happy or an unhappy year? We may search far and wide before we find any such person. No, every year will be the result of what we make it, the result of something that we put into operation this minute. It will not do to wait until midnight tonight; it will not do to wait until tomorrow. The kind of year that we are to experience must be started now, in this moment, by an act of decision, and each one must make that decision for himself.

This moment we must choose whether we will serve God or man. Are we to be God-governed or man-governed this year? If we are true to God, we need have no fear that we will be untrue to man, to our government, or to any government that stands for individual freedom, liberty, justice, and for the integrity of individual being. Therefore, we take our stand for government under God.

But what does government under God mean? First of all, it means that we must acknowledge that God has given to us His only begotten Son, and the function of this Presence that has been planted in the midst of us is to go before us to "make the crooked places straight." [8] It is to go before us to prepare mansions for us.

Now Is the Power and the Dominion

In making this acknowledgment, we are at the same time forsaking our dependence on "man, whose breath is in his nostrils." [9]

[8] Isaiah 45:2.
[9] Isaiah 2:22.

We will not seek the favor of "princes": we will understand that this son of God in us is there for the specific purpose of doing the will of God in us; and this will of God, as demonstrated in the ministry of the Master, is that we might have life, health, and joy, and that we might have all these more abundantly.

If we are to have dominion, we must acknowledge that there are no powers antagonistic to the son of God in us, for the power of God is infinite, and besides this spiritual power there is no power. Every day of every year we will be faced with the temptation to accept material, mental, and legal powers; but at this moment we must embrace in our acknowledgment the great truth that God is Spirit, that the law of God is spiritual, and being spiritual, it is infinite; and being infinite, there is no power in any law other than the spiritual law which is embodied within us.

This son of God, the *I* [10] that I am, is our food, shelter, protection, fortress, hiding place, and our abiding place, embodying all the good necessary to our experience throughout the years. At this very moment, we possess all that will unfold as our experience for all the days to come: it is embodied and embraced within our consciousness, and day by day it will unfold and appear as necessary in our human experience. All that God has is ours now.

Our Consciousness of Today Molds Our Tomorrows

Every new minute is a continuation of this present minute, and what we put into this minute is what is going to be a continuing experience for us throughout eternity. All that is embraced in our consciousness now will continue to unfold unto eternity because there is no future time. Now, in the present, is the substance of that which unfolds to us as time, and it includes that

[10] The word *"I,"* italicized, refers to God.

which we are placing in it at this moment. What we embody in our consciousness now unfolds as the next minute, the next hour, the next day, the next year. The truth that we embody in consciousness at this moment will be the continuing, unfolding truth throughout all time. What we do not embrace in our consciousness now cannot appear tomorrow.

"For he that hath, to him shall be given: and he that hath not, from him shall be taken even that which he hath." [11] Therefore, we must make certain that now, in this instant, we claim for ourselves all that the Father has, and that not by might, not by power, but by the grace of God, as heirs, as joint-heirs to all that God has. But if we do not consciously claim it now, we will not have it tomorrow. We will have tomorrow only what we claim today, now, in this moment.

Do we have the life of God? Then we have immortal, eternal life. Do we have the Spirit of God? Then we have the spirit of freedom, for "where the Spirit of the Lord is, there is liberty." [12] Only under the grace of God and His law can man be free. What we have in our consciousness of God-realization this moment will continue to flow day by day, and in ever greater measure as we renew ourselves many times a day by turning within to the Source of our good, thereby releasing the kingdom of God that is within.

The Inseparability of God and Man

Let us see how we can make this more practical in our experience, and why it is that no person or circumstance can deprive us of health, wealth, harmony, joy, and freedom. Let us rise, right now, to the realization that will forever set us free. You can do this by asking yourself two questions: Who am I? What am

[11] Mark 4:25.
[12] II Corinthians 3:17.

I? With your eyes closed, and in complete silence, say the word "I" within yourself, following it by your own name, whatever it may be. Then, with your eyes still closed, ask yourself: Am I in my feet? Am I in my stomach? Am I in my brain? You know that you are not. You know that the *I* of you cannot be found any place between your head and your feet.

> *I am God-created, and since God is Spirit, I must be spiritual. God is invisible, and therefore, I must be invisible: I can never be seen by anyone. I am as invisible, as spiritual, and as incorporeal as God, for this I that I am is the offspring of God, made of the life, substance, and being of God.*

It is for this reason that even when we lay aside our earthly form, *I,* in Its full identity, will continue. Being one with God, *I* is inseparable and indivisible from God, and not even death can remove us from the life of God or the love of God, for our life and God-life are one.

> *God-life and my life are one, inseparable, indivisible, and incorporeal, not at the mercy of "man, whose breath is in his nostrils," not at the mercy of "princes," but a divine life lived under God.*
>
> *"I and my Father are one,"* [13] *incorporeal and invisible. I live, and move, and have my being in God; I live and have my being in Spirit, in the Soul of God, in the Spirit of God. I am hid with Christ in God: this is my fortress; this is my dwelling place—to live, move, and have my being in Spirit, under spiritual government.*

To acknowledge the life of God as our life reveals our life as immortal and eternal. To acknowledge God as the substance, even of our body, makes our body indestructible, not subject to age or change, to sin, disease, or fear.

[13] John 10:30.

Consciousness Is I

As we silently repeat *I,* together with our name, we may begin to wonder about the nature of this *I* that we are, and soon the one thing we can be sure of is that we are a state of awareness or consciousness. In other words, we are conscious of living, of thinking, of moving about; we are conscious of the world in which we live; and through what we have read, heard, or studied, we are conscious of other worlds, other countries, other nationalities, and other languages. Therefore, we are consciousness.

Sight is one of the avenues of consciousness. Because we are consciousness, we are conscious of things by seeing them. We are also conscious of things by hearing; and hearing, therefore, is an extension or an activity of consciousness. It is consciousness that is conscious, but it is consciously aware through the activities or instruments of our consciousness: sight, hearing, taste, touch, and smell. These five senses, plus our capacity to think, are extensions, or outer activities, of the consciousness which we are.

Is it not clear that this *I* that we have declared ourselves to be is really consciousness? *I* is consciousness, or consciousness constitutes the *I* that we are. Therefore, what we are as consciousness is what becomes our experience. If we are conscious of the truth that there is only one infinite Consciousness, by virtue of our relationship of oneness with God, that infinite Consciousness, God, must be our individual consciousness; and that makes us as infinite as God, as immortal and as eternal.

God As Individual Consciousness

There is not an infinite Consciousness and your and my consciousness, otherwise there would be Infinity plus something,
which cannot be. Therefore, the infinite Consciousness which is
God is the consciousness which we are. Because of our oneness
with God, we, individually, have access to the infinite nature of
God's being, to the infinite, eternal life of God. God is consciousness; we are that Consciousness individualized; but that
Consciousness is one consciousness, indivisible, indestructible,
immortal, eternal, and above all things, omnipresent, here where
we are, and It [14] is omnipotent.

Because God is our Selfhood, God is the measure of our capacity. Infinite Being is the nature of our being; infinite Being is
the capacity of our being; and now, in this moment, we must
recognize, acknowledge, and submit ourselves to It. As we remind ourselves of this each day, then this particular moment of
our life, which we are now making happy, joyous, and prosperous, becomes the continuing moment of every day of every year.
This no man can take from us. Even we ourselves will not be
able to limit it to one day or to one year. It will be the joy and
prosperity of all the years to come on this side of the veil or the
other, for neither life nor death can separate us from the love of
God, the life and the consciousness of God, the awareness which
is now our being.

God is consciousness, therefore, there can be but one Consciousness, and the fact that we are conscious is proof that
the Consciousness which is God is our individual consciousness.

[14] In the spiritual literature of the world, the varying concepts of **God**
are indicated by the use of such words as "Father," "Mother," "Soul,"
"Spirit," "Principle," "Love," "Life." Therefore, in this book the author
has used the pronouns "He" and "It," or "Himself" and "Itself" inter-
changeably in referring to **God**.

We, therefore, have access to unlimited wisdom, power, dominion, and law. Since God is the life of all this universe—and no one as yet has discovered a form of life separate and apart from the universal Life which is God—this Life then is our life. Our life and the Father's life are one. The Life which is God is the Life which is man: one Life, eternal, immortal, spiritual. God is the lawgiver. Then there can be only one law, and that is the law of God, and if we come in contact with material law, legal or economic law, it is our responsibility to realize that it has no power except as it is of the law of God: spiritual, harmonious, abundant, and infinite.

Daily Sowing and Reaping

"I"—the Spirit of God—"am come that they might have life, and that they might have it more abundantly." [15] That abundant life is ours when we live, and move, and have our being hid with Christ in God, where the universal beliefs of "this world" cannot intrude, nor enter to defile or to make a lie.

When we know the truth, then the truth can operate and make us free, and the truth that we are to know is that *I,* the presence of God, the consciousness of God, the life of God, is come in the midst of us that we might have life, and that we might have it more abundantly, freely, and joyously, and that we might share it with all those who are in spiritual darkness. It is not ours to keep; it is not ours to hide in a mountaintop or in some remote ashrama or temple. We may retire to such a place for a week or for forty days of inner contemplation, but we must come down to the plains, down to the seashore, yes, down even to the valley to share with the people of this world who are not yet enlightened and who, therefore, are not yet aware of their destiny of freedom under God. With those whom we find receptive and

[15] John 10:10.

responsive, we must share this great secret of the oneness of our individual being, and theirs, with the infinite and eternal Source.

Let us pour out our gifts of the Spirit to the multitudes; but let us never seek the multitudes. We do not go up and down the highways and byways, even of our family, trying to find somebody upon whom to force this gift; because if we squander the gift of the Spirit on the unprepared thought, we shall find ourselves depleted. We wait for the multitudes to come to us. Should the multitudes consist of only one person, we wait for that one to come to us. We sit quietly at home, or in our shop or office, with our finger on our lips, keeping our treasure hidden from the world. Those who are receptive respond to the light within us, and recognize the glint in our eyes, or the smile on our face. As they come, one by one, let us accept each one as the multitude. They come to us for bread, which we give them, and cold water and warm water, too. We give them what they are seeking. We give it to them gently; we give it to them gradually; we give it to them with love, with joy, and with the power of authority. We can draw upon the infinity of our being, and anything will flow: words of truth, compassion, love, healing, grace, finances, food, water, drink, protection, care, companionship—all these will flow forth from the Christ within us.[16]

"Whatsoever a man soweth, that shall he also reap." [17] As we sow now to the Spirit, so will we reap life everlasting. If we waste our time in sowing to the flesh, we will reap corruption. But now, in this moment, which is to be the continuing moment of the year to come, we are sowing to the Spirit, sowing to the truth, sowing to life eternal, sowing to spiritual freedom under God's grace. Then will come the reaping and the sharing.

Let us daily remember the spiritual nature of our being, and at least once every day close our eyes and silently repeat to ourselves that word *I,* followed by our name, and then pause to realize the incorporeal, indestructible nature of our being. The incorporeal, invisible nature of the Father is the incorporeal, in-

[16] From the author's *The Art of Meditation* (New York: Harper and Brothers, 1956), pp. 90, 91.
[17] Galatians 6:7.

visible nature of the *I* that we are, and all that the Father has is ours unto eternity. Neither life nor death can separate us from the allness of God.

Living Love Is Living the God-Life

To pray for our enemies, our friends, and for our relatives is to know the truth. This truth that we have been knowing is the universal truth about all God's creation. It is not the truth about mortal man because mortal man is living in defiance of the laws of God. It is true only of that *I* that is living in conscious one-ness with God, and we are living in that conscious oneness only when we are living the life of love, loving our neighbor as our-selves, loving our fellow man, forgiving even our persecutors and enemies.

The mortal life is not of God: it is destructible. The life that is lived in the belief in good and evil is not under the law of God, and only when we live forgiveness, live in sharing and giving, are we living the God-life, that incorporeal, spiritual life that is in-destructible, the life that not even flames can destroy or swords pierce.

This life which we bring to our remembrance when we realize the true meaning of *I* is our God-given, immortal life, and we live it through love, and only through love. When selfishness, greed, lust, animality, hate, envy, and jealousy are permitted en-trance into our consciousness, we are living a life apart from God, a life which has no support from God, and therefore a life which must come to an end.

We can reject that human sense of life by renouncing the per-sonal sense of self which is characterized by a lack of love, a lack of justice, or a lack of benevolence; and we can accept the *I* that is one with God, the *I* that is the Spirit of God that has come as our individual being that we might have life, and that we might share this life through love and forgiveness, by releasing everyone from all obligations to us, through praying for others, and through knowing the truth.

"Owe no man any thing, but to love one another: for he that loveth another hath fulfilled the law.[18] . . . This is my commandment, That ye love one another, as I have loved you." [19] Love—this is the heritage, this is the nature of the *I* that we are.

> *Since "I and my Father are one," my whole reliance is on Him, on the* I *that I am, the Consciousness that I am, the Consciousness that embraces within Itself infinity.*
>
> *I am conscious through sight, through hearing, through taste, touch, and smell. I am conscious through thinking: I am consciousness itself.*
>
> *In the consciousness that I am are embraced the whole universe and all the worlds to come, for the consciousness which I am and the Consciousness which God is are one and the same consciousness. All that the Father has is mine; all that God is as Consciousness, I am as consciousness, for I am that* I AM.

"He that hath seen me hath seen the Father." [20] If we can see the *I* of individual being—Consciousness, incorporeal, spiritual Being—we are seeing God, that *I* that is one with the Father. Let us remember always that when we are outwardly and openly saying, "Good morning," or wishing anyone a happy New Year, inwardly we are adding:

> I, *the Father within you, give unto you a good morning or a happy New Year.* I, *in the midst of you, give unto you* My *peace.* God's *morning, God's New Year, give* I *unto you.*

ACROSS THE DESK

Everyone is surrounded to some extent by human love, care, consideration, and resources, but until we think about it, we

18 Romans 13:8.
19 John 15:12.
20 John 14:9.

may not fully appreciate how much human good we are enjoying. What we receive from parents, husband, wife, children, and friends, we usually take for granted, or we tend to dwell so much on our nagging lacks that we do not fully realize the gifts, inheritances, and blessings we are continually receiving.

At some time or other on his spiritual journey, this is brought to the attention of the spiritual seeker. It is often when his human resources fail him that the budding mystic is born because now he must turn his attention to spiritual resources, to the Kingdom within himself.

There are those who under the stress and strain of a period of barrenness fall away and are lost for this lifetime at least. Others can go through the period of human desertion and material lack and gradually shift the base of their dependence from the outer to the inner realm of consciousness. These are the ones in whom that Something within has been awakened; these are the budding mystics who know that He "hangeth the earth upon nothing," [21] that He that is within them is greater than he that is in the world. These are the few who finally reach the realization that "I have meat to eat that ye know not of." [22]

With this understanding, the transition from the man of earth to that man who has his being in Christ begins to be made. "The natural man receiveth not the things of the Spirit of God," [23] and as long as man lives secure in, and content with, his human relationships and material resources he is "not subject to the law of God, neither indeed can be." [24]

When, however, he becomes aware of the clinging to, and dependence on, "man, whose breath is in his nostrils," [25] and begins consciously to change his base of reliance to the Nothingness which constitutes spiritual Presence and Power, he begins to bud spiritually and eventually must bear fruit richly.

[21] Job 26:7.
[22] John 4:32.
[23] I Corinthians 2:14.
[24] Romans 8:7.
[25] Isaiah 2:22.

A mystic lives in something like a shell of Nothingness: he feels no dependence on outer circumstance, person, or condition; he feels no fear of external powers, whether appearing as person or condition. He lives in a sense of Self-completeness, sustained first by the realization that "I have meat to eat that ye know not of" [26] and finally by the conscious awareness that "I am the way, the truth, and the life.[27] . . . I am the resurrection." [28]

The mystic, having attained spiritual Grace, finds himself well endowed materially and mentally as well as spiritually, and therefore has "twelve baskets full" to share.

[26] John 4:32.
[27] John 14:6.
[28] John 11:25.

Barriers to Spiritual Attainment

———•———

As human beings we all want or need something, and it is the desire for that something that blocks our spiritual development. It is the desire or need for something apart from God that sets up within us a sense of separation from Him, or leads us to believe that we could be satisfied with something other than the presence and power of God.

The very desire for something good, something as good as to be of service, is a barrier to spiritual development for we have no right to want anything, even to want to do good. We have only one right: to want to know God. Then, if God places us in some form of service—teaching, healing, nursing, painting, writing plays or books, or whatever it may be—we perform our work with joy and gladness because we are permitting ourselves to be transparencies through which God can shine. But for us to desire to do any of these things would be to glorify ourselves, and that is wrong.

It is difficult to live the spiritual life because in the human picture we are continuously desiring something—to be something, to do something, to benefit or to bless someone—and that is the barrier to spiritual development. The dissolving of the barrier comes with the relinquishment of our desires, wants, wishes, or outlining, so that we can go to God pure, not asking for supply, companionship, or to be of service, but asking only that God's grace be established in us, that God envelop and permeate us, that we may come to know Him aright, realize our oneness with Him, and thereby become consciously one with the creative Principle of our being. That is all. We, then, have no further needs, no further wants, no further desires.

The Fruitage of Conscious Oneness with God

To live in conscious union with God draws to us all that is necessary to fulfill our experience as long as we do not outline what that experience is to be or desire it to unfold in some particular way. That union with God, acting through us, forces us into the particular activity that will be of the greatest service to others and brings the greatest fulfillment to us.

Our conscious oneness with God constitutes our oneness with every spiritual idea and with every form of life.[1] Behind every form of nature, there is spiritual life, and when we are consciously one with God, we are consciously and instantaneously one with the life of every plant and animal—not with their physical life, but with their spiritual life. As long as they are a part of our consciousness, they will partake of our consciousness, and

[1] For a further exposition of this subject, see the author's *Conscious Union With God* (New York: Julian Press, 1962).

our consciousness of truth will be their resurrected and renewed life.

Our consciousness of God becomes the consciousness of our patients and students. As long as they are in our consciousness, they are partaking of our understanding; they are eating of the bread, meat, wine, and water which is our realized consciousness of truth, and our consciousness of our oneness with God becomes a law of harmony unto them.

Being Single-Minded

Thousands of students all over the world who maintain contact with The Infinite Way consciousness, either through the monthly *Letter,* reading the books, hearing the tapes, or attending Infinite Way meetings where there is an uplifted consciousness, find that they go through years and years with little or no disease or discord. For long periods of time, they have few problems of a serious nature, and those that do arise dissolve more readily.

This is not always true in the first, second, or third year of study because beginning students have not yet learned how to make contact with the higher Consciousness, and they are still engrossed in living their own lives. They have not accepted themselves as a part of The Infinite Way consciousness, and they are, therefore, living part of their life following The Infinite Way and part of it with some other form of metaphysics or sometimes with six different forms. Such students do not wholeheartedly embrace the principles of any particular teaching, and consequently their consciousness is united with nothing.

From the moment a student realizes that The Infinite Way is his way of life and has united himself with it, he begins to find that The Infinite Way consciousness itself maintains his freedom for him. "And I, if I be lifted up from the earth, will draw all men unto me:" [2] I, if I be lifted into God-consciousness, will lift those who come to me to that same state of consciousness, and they will then partake of its fruitage.

The Master placed a condition on the continuous enjoyment of that fruitage when he said, "Behold, thou art made whole: sin no more, lest a worse thing come unto thee." [3] In other words, we must not go back to the state of consciousness in which we originally were, because it can bear only the same kind of fruit. Now that we have been lifted into a higher consciousness, we must be sure that we continue acting out from that consciousness. Before we knew the truth, we could do many things that brought no penalty upon us because we had not touched the higher, more rarified consciousness.

But now we cannot afford to be untrue to our highest sense of integrity or to violate the least important spiritual law—not even to accept appearances at face value—without paying a penalty for it. In the degree that we come down from that high sense in the slightest measure, we suffer. That is because we have become so sensitive and so attuned to the Spirit that coarse or evil thoughts or actions react very quickly upon us.

Give Up Seeking Forms of Good

To sow to the flesh has a far deeper meaning than the usual meaning the world has given it. If in any way we put our faith in form rather than in the essence or substance of the form, in that degree are we going to bear only material fruitage, which is corruption.

No matter what we achieve or possess humanly—whether a fortune, a marriage, or a healthy physical body—it is subject to deterioration and death; in fact, it is dying from the time of birth. Anything that is acquired humanly has only the substance

[2] John 12:32.
[3] John 5:14.

of itself and is bound by its own limitations. If, through our conscious oneness with God, however, some good comes into our experience—money, home, marriage, companionship, employment, or service—it is an until-death-do-us-part relationship, an eternal relationship. We can never be separated from any good that comes to us through our conscious oneness with God.

If we can go through lack of any nature and are able to stand fast, not seeking to demonstrate persons, things, or conditions, but seeking only to demonstrate conscious union with God, the substance of all form, then the supply of whatever is lacking will unfold.

Some students who experience a temporary sense of economic lack are unable to rest in a complete reliance on the Spirit when their situation becomes acute, and they resort to human manipulation and conniving, thereby losing their whole demonstration of spiritual living. Other students to whom economic abundance comes very soon after they have entered the spiritual path become so fascinated with the money that is accumulated or with the things that money can buy that they also lose their demonstration. It is not money that makes or loses the demonstration, nor is it a lack of money. Nothing in the outer form is the determining factor: what counts is conscious union with God.

Many a person has had to come to death's door before he found God, and he could not find God until he reached that point. Why? He was trying to find health, and as long as a person is trying to find health, he will not find God. He must give up the search for forms and realize that health is not all-important, and that if he had all the health there is in the world today, it could turn into sickness tomorrow.

As a matter of fact, what difference does it make how healthy, youthful, beautiful, or handsome we are as long as the passage of time will inevitably change this so that the picture is completely reversed? What point is there, then, in taking pride in youth, health, or wealth? They are all fleeting.

But if we make God our goal, realizing that nothing is going to satisfy us except conscious union with God, there will never be such things as age, lack, loneliness, or emptiness in our experience. In God's presence is the fulfillment of life, and there is no other way to attain real fulfillment. In the presence of God, there is joy: freedom from every form of lack.

The Continuity of Life Is Not Dependent on Processes

Another step forward in our spiritual development is taken when we come to the place where we are not demanding that life fulfill itself on this side of the grave, because now we are not desiring this or that side, but only fulfillment. If the Spirit of God dwell in us, then do we have the capacity to release our desires, even the desire for human life, as we realize: "What possible difference can it make whether I am looking at life from this side or that? As far as God is concerned, does it matter on which side of the border life is being lived? Life is eternal: it cannot be otherwise. It is going on continuously and fulfilling itself without end."

> *Nothing do I seek—nothing. The realization of my conscious oneness with God is enough. In my oneness with God, I am one with all spiritual life everywhere: on this side of the grave, the other side, and the side of life that has not yet come into manifestation in this world.*

All space is filled with the life of God, all space and all time—past, present, and future—and we are one with that life, even one with that which is unborn. Life exists before birth, and life exists during and after birth, and life exists after death because God is life and God is the only life.

There is no power that can prevent the life of God from expressing. The life of God lives to express itself. We can hold it back, however, by the belief that it is dependent on physical organs or functions. But the life of God is Spirit, and that needs no material aids to sustain it. Therefore, the life of God can express itself whithersoever it will, and it does. But it is up to us to remove the barriers that would claim that it is dependent upon a process, dependent on an organ or on a function. Life is dependent on God's grace, and on God's grace alone. When God's grace wants the life of God to appear, it appears.

Conscious Oneness with God Brings Fulfillment

To be consciously one with God is to be consciously one with the spiritual life of all being and all form; therefore, whatever is necessary to our fulfillment will come into our experience. If it is patients to be healed or students to be taught, they will find us; if it is pictures to be painted, or books to be written, if it is marriage, family, or business, it will all flow out into expression. Nothing can stop God from fulfilling Itself, once we have made contact with God. If we do not make contact with God, God is still fulfilling Itself—but not in our experience.

Harmonious and successful living depends on one demonstration alone: the demonstration of conscious oneness with God. If a person comes to us with a problem and if we can become consciously one with God, that oneness with God appears in his life as the experience he needs, even though we may not know what that need is, and he, himself, may not know what it is. All he knows is the lack he feels, but we do not know, nor can we know, the way fulfillment will appear in any particular situation.

In The Infinite Way, it makes no difference what the nature of the problem is. One person may have a fever, another one chills; one may have a growth, and another a lack of substance. All we have to do to help him is to become consciously one with God, and whatever the nature of his need is, it is met. If fulfillment must come in less flesh or more flesh, it will; if it has to demonstrate itself in more companionship or less companionship, it will.

Letting the Divine Intelligence Operate in Human Relationships

Whatever the form of the need, divine Intelligence takes care of the whole matter without our interposing our beliefs. This underscores the point that a practitioner should never give human advice when he is called upon for help. For example, in marital affairs, he should never advise separation, divorce, or a continuation of the marriage. He must have no opinion about it at all: he must make conscious contact with God, and let God do to the life of that couple what It will. If their life will best be fulfilled together, all the obstacles to that togetherness will be removed. If, on the other hand, it is necessary for them to be separated to find individual fulfillment, this consciously realized Spirit will bring about the separation quickly and painlessly without loss to either one. If the practitioner enters such a case with a preconceived notion of what the demonstration should be, he is operating on the level of a marriage counselor or a psychological adviser, and that is not spiritual healing.

A practitioner's function is not to determine whether a person should be married, single, or divorced, whether he should live in this city or that city, or in this country or that country. The practitioner's function is to go to God, make conscious union with God, and then let the presence of God do what It will.

The Realization of God's Presence, the One Essential

The principle of attaining conscious oneness with God is effective in every activity of life. When I am giving a lecture or conducting a class, I never go to God for a message. When I meditate, it is for the realization of God's presence, and when I attain that, God's presence provides the message. If I should go to God for a message, I would be going for an effect or for a form, and I would lose the essence. As long as I do not seek for a message, but desire only the presence of God, it is the presence of God that will speak and give the message that is to come through me.

Much of what is in my books, I myself did not know until it came flowing out, and I was taught at the same time the students were. I have no way of gaining knowledge except as it comes through inspiration. So, from experience, I have learned not to want messages, not to want patients, and not to want students.

One thing alone do I want and need: the feeling and the awareness of God's presence, the consciousness of my oneness with God. Let me feel that God is living my life, and I will trust myself to go around the world without purse or scrip, or into any class without a message. Just let me feel that God is holding my hand, that the presence of God is with me, and, like Daniel, I will not fear lions either—but I would want to be sure that I had God right there beside me, or I could be very much frightened by a harmless little pussy-cat.

If we make our conscious contact with God, our life will be fulfilled according to God's plan, not according to our outline of what it should be, and God's plan usually turns out to be much better than anything we could have planned.

There is no such thing as personal power, and those who believe there is sooner or later find a power greater than themselves and are sometimes broken by it. Even leaning on God for something can be dangerous because, too many times, it is not God on whom we are leaning but on an idea in our mind, a belief, or a concept of God, and we cannot afford to lean on that. The only thing we can lean on is Nothingness: nothing we know, nothing we can see, hear, taste, touch, or smell. On That we can lean. And we will not really have to lean: we will be resting in the Is-ness of God.

"For my thoughts are not your thoughts, neither are your ways my ways.[4] . . . My peace I give unto you: not as the world giveth, give I unto you." [5] God's thoughts and God's peace transcend human understanding, but they come only to the person who has made conscious union with God. In that union, all things appear in the outer world.

Losing Fear of Effects

The correct letter of truth, taken into our consciousness, thought about, pondered and meditated upon, lived with, and practiced, develops a spiritual state of consciousness. We can see how this practice becomes realized consciousness if we take the basic premise that there is no power in form or effect and work with it.

This principle might be tested by placing money in front of us and then watching to see whether there is any power in it. Immediately, we observe that it stays where we put it, and there it will stay forever and forever and forever—just dead. It has no power; it cannot go out and buy even a cup of coffee; it cannot draw interest; it cannot multiply itself. It cannot come to me, and it cannot go to you. The minute this is perceived, we can relax and give up the struggle for it. Is something as dead as this piece of metal or paper in front of us worth struggling for?

[4] Isaiah 55:8.
[5] John 14:27.

Power is not in money: the power is in supply, the invisible Spirit of God, the Intelligence or Love that is within us. That Spirit of God draws the form of supply to us. It will maintain it, and the Spirit of God within us will intelligently and lovingly make use of it. Now we can use money as a tool or an instrument because the Intelligence that brought it to us is the Intelligence that knows what to do with it and can spend or invest it. It is not money that is worth struggling about: it is the spiritual wisdom that brings it to us that is worth achieving.

Money is an instrument or form of supply; it is the outer expression of supply, but it is not supply. Every time any thought of needing money, food, clothing, or housing comes to us, we should remember: "That is not supply. That is the form of supply, but supply itself is infinite and omnipresent, because God is supply. God is infinite, God is omnipresent, and wherever I am, God is; therefore, I have an infinity of supply."

Repeating this or reading it will not make it come to pass. It will become realized consciousness only if we ponder it, think about it, if each day we continue to remind ourselves that we have supply, and if each day the idea that money is power becomes deader and deader to us. We do not even have to pray for supply. The whole kingdom of God is established in us, and even God cannot withhold or take it from us because infinity is the measure of our supply.

Gradually our consciousness changes from one that places reliance on money to one that has an understanding of the omnipresence of supply, and thereby we develop the spiritual consciousness of supply. It may take a week, a month, or a year before this is completely attained. It will not take that long, however, to make a beginning. Within a short time, we shall find that we are losing our fear of lack. Our fear and our love of money are diminishing, because now we are beginning to see that, in and of itself, money is dead, just a form to be used. That changes our consciousness.

Losing the Material Sense of Body

In the area of health, also, harmony depends on our demonstration of God. There are persons suffering with diseases, and behind that suffering is the belief that harmony is dependent on some function or organ of the body. All human life is built on that premise. If anything happens to the heart, we die; if anything happens to the digestion or elimination, we become sick. We have to reverse that. Life is God, so life is not dependent on heart, liver, or lungs. Heart, liver, and lungs are dependent on life. It is life that beats the heart. It is life that activates the liver, the digestion, the elimination, and the muscles. It is not the body that moves life: it is life that moves the body, and life we are.

As long as we can say, "I am," we exist, we have life, and that life governs the body. As we maintain that, we lose the materialistic consciousness of body as governing life, and we attain the spiritual awareness of life governing the body.

"Man shall not live by bread alone." [6] Man shall not live by form or effect, whether it is baker's bread or butcher's meat, or the form that we call heart, liver, or lungs. Man shall not live by effect, but "by every word that proceedeth out of the mouth of God." [7] When we realize that the word of God is our life, the life of our being and of our body, our whole consciousness begins to change, and we stop fearing the organs and functions of the body. Through this practice, a new consciousness is being developed.

[6] Matthew 4:4.
[7] *Ibid.*

Releasing Desire

The barriers to our spiritual progress are our hopes, ambitions, and desires, even when they are good. Some of us cannot release the quest for health, and others cannot release the seeking for rent, food, clothing, or companionship. Always one of these lacks or desires is the thing that we feel must be solved first. We believe that if we could just be rid of our pain, then we could seek God; or if we could demonstrate more supply, then we could think of God. No, it works in reverse: if we think of God first, we will have all these other things. "Man, whose breath is in his nostrils" [8] must always want things, conditions, or persons, and therefore he is never free to seek the kingdom of God and His righteousness.

We may want to be given a thought with which to do healing work, but that is an effect. We may want to be given a truth about supply or companionship, but that, too, is an effect. Even desiring good thoughts is desiring effects. We do not desire good thoughts: we desire only one thing: peace, peace, peace.

Desire is always the barrier to our progress, and certainly a barrier to the attainment of meditation. When we reach a point where there is nothing we want to gain from meditation, where we are not going into meditation for any purpose, but just turning within to be still, meditation is easy to attain. It is only when we take into our meditation our desire for some thing, and such a desire is a desire for an effect, that that inner stillness and peace of meditation elude us.

Working with the principles that constitute the letter of truth develops the spirit or consciousness of truth. Eventually we are living in Christ-consciousness where it is very easy to meditate because we have neither hate, fear, nor love of anything in the external realm. Even our love for friends and family takes on a

[8] Isaiah 2:22.

spiritual nature, which brings about in them a change toward us so that they do not cling to us as they once did, or depend or rely upon us.

The realization that God is the fulfillment of our being sets them and us free to love because we are free to give and receive without any clinging or attachment. We can love our families without believing they owe us anything and without feeling we owe them anything but to love them. They have the same God we have, and now we are united in a closer bond than we ever were before: we are united in that bond of love which can freely give and freely receive, and never feel that in giving we have deprived ourselves of anything or that in receiving we have deprived anyone else of anything.

To come to the realization of our oneness with God is the most freeing experience in the world. But we come to it by practicing and practicing and practicing, and by holding to this truth until gradually our whole consciousness changes. When it does, and this world becomes "dead" to us, we have won the whole world: it is all ours then, every single bit of it. It was only the desire for it that kept it away. There is now nothing to be achieved, nothing to be gained, nothing to be won. All already is. The Lord already is our shepherd, not because we earn or deserve it, or are worthy, not because we are going to do anything, but just because the Lord is our shepherd, and we shall not want.

Gain the conscious realization of the presence and power of God within your own being. Regardless of the name or nature of the problem or need, do not try to solve it on the level of the problem. Do not try to solve supply as supply; do not try to solve family relationships as family relationships. Drop all thought of these things. Go within until you actually find that place within your being which gives you the God-response. Then your problems will be solved. Once you have touched the Christ within your own being, you have touched the wellspring of life more abundant.

*Conscious oneness with God! This constitutes conscious one-
ness with all spiritual being and with every spiritual idea.*[9]

ACROSS THE DESK

It was in 1947 that the first edition of *The Infinite Way* was
published. Today it is in its eleventh edition, and it and the
many other Infinite Way writings since then have traveled the
world in American and British editions, and some in German,
Dutch, French, and Japanese. Fifteen years ago, I was the only
Infinite Way student in the world, and now see what God hath
wrought around the globe! Only God could produce such a miracle.

It is becoming increasingly clear to me that God is permeating
human consciousness with His presence and His grace. Each
one of us as an Infinite Way student is His love and His life in
action: "I live; yet not I, but Christ liveth in me." [10] Each one of
us must realize that Truth is living in us for Its purpose.

"Ye have not chosen me, but I have chosen you." [11] Neither
you nor I chose this Way, but we have been chosen that God's
grace may be made visible on earth through us. Through us,
God's plan is being revealed, and His will is being done on earth
as it is in heaven.

Just as God has always chosen as His temples, teachers, disciples, apostles, and students, so today, God has chosen those
men and women dedicated to conscious union with Him to appear as the temple of Truth evidenced all over the world. Those
who abide in meditation experience His presence and thereby
release into consciousness His grace and peace. "I can of mine
own self do nothing," [12] but "I can do all things through Christ

[9] By the author. *Conscious Union With God* (New York: Julian Press,
1962). pp. 252-253.
[10] Galatians 2:20.
[11] John 15:16.
[12] John 5:30.

which strengtheneth me." [13] Except we be chosen of God, we cannot fulfill His mission, and we are chosen when we feel His Spirit within us.

"But the natural man receiveth not the things of the Spirit of God" [14]—only those in whom His Spirit consciously dwells. "Ye shall know them by their fruits," [15] and hereby do we know if His Spirit dwells in us: if we bring His grace and His peace with us in whatever place in life we walk. We need not leave our homes or our business, but we must carry into these His comfort, healing, and peace.

Let us always be recognized by our awareness that the joy and peace we bring are His. "If I bear witness of myself, my witness is not true": [16] it is the Father's will that comforts, heals, blesses, and multiplies. By His grace are we the light that His will may be done, not man's will or man's thought.

Looking out at the world, we see His light shining in the face of man. Looking at the events of the world, we witness more and more of His will and His grace. The Infinite Way again reveals the kingdom of God on earth, the will of God in man, and the grace of God come as peace in the heart of man.

We have not chosen this or done this, but the Father has chosen the time and the way.

[13] Philippians 4:13.
[14] I Corinthians 2:14.
[15] Matthew 7:16.
[16] John 5:31.

When the Spirit of the Lord Is Upon Us

———•———

The goal of our journey on the spiritual path is to make the transition from being the man of earth who is not under the law of God to being that man who has his being in Christ, to leave behind that selfhood which is sometimes good and sometimes bad, sometimes sick and sometimes well, sometimes rich and sometimes poor, and to emerge into our divine state as a child of God.

According to the Master, we are either branches that are one with the tree of Life or branches that are cut off from the tree. If we are branches that are cut off, we are withering and dying; but if we are connected with the trunk, then we are one with the entire tree and all that constitutes the tree, way down into the roots and coming up through the roots. We are at-one with all that is in the soil, with the sunshine and with the rain. Everything that seeps down into the soil comes up through the roots, feeds the whole tree, and then produces the fruitage.

The Road Back to the Father's House

Every problem with which we are faced stems from a separation from our Source, and until we are once again united with that Source, troubles are going to continue to recur in our minds and bodies. Both the mind and the body have to be fed. For centuries, it was considered sufficient if the body were fed and maintained with food, medicine, and fresh air; but in the last hundred years it has been discovered that we need something more than that, and so attempts have been made to teach people to fill their minds with thoughts of a positive nature on the assumption that the body would in turn respond to this constructive approach to life. But if we are not fed by the Spirit, all the material food we can put into our systems will not feed us properly, nor will all the mental food with which we fill the mind give us adequate nourishment.

As human beings, we have no contact with our Soul, or Source, and it is only when we begin the practice of meditation that we find our way back to the Father's house. The story of the Prodigal Son, unless it is correctly understood, might indicate that the journey back to the Father's house was merely a physical act, and that is not true. The banquet with the swine is nothing more nor less than the life we are living day by day separate and apart from God, and the return to the Father's house is a journey that has to be taken, not by going any place physically but by an act of consciousness.

This act of consciousness can never take place until there is the recognition that we have been wandering in a far country, in a land of physicality and mentality, and that it is necessary for us to make the return journey back to the Father's house, a journey which is accomplished within ourselves as an activity of consciousness. That activity of consciousness is meditation.

Practice, Practice, Practice

When we meditate, although in the beginning nothing may seem to be taking place, from the very first time we made the effort, an inner stirring was going on, even though it may have been so slight as to be imperceptible. It is very much like taking piano lessons and practicing diligently for a half hour or an hour, and then at the end of that time, when we find that we cannot play the piano, we think that nothing has happened. Even on the second or the third day, we may observe no noticeable progress. If, however, we persist for sixty, ninety, or a hundred and twenty days, we can see the progress we have made, progress which has been going on from that very first day.

So it is with meditation. We may meditate many times a day, and at the end of a month feel that we have made no visible progress. But if we could know what can happen by the end of a year, we would understand why it took every one of those attempts at meditation to attain even a measure of conscious oneness with the Source of life, and thereby become like the branch of a tree that has been grafted back onto the tree.

Becoming Universal Through Uniting with the Source

Every bit of rain that falls, every bit of sunshine, every bit of snow that enriches the soil is sent up through the roots into the tree, feeding the trunk, finding its way through the trunk into the branches, and then finally becoming buds and blossoms and fruit. The branch has no awareness of the many sources that are feeding it, and yet it is benefiting by all of them.

We may not be aware of the invisible forces that are contrib-
uting to our physical, mental, moral, financial, and spiritual wel-
fare, or even of the people around the world who are playing an
unseen and unknown part in our development. But just as everything that is drawn up through the trunk of the tree from any
source helps feed every individual branch, so this oneness with
God, attained through meditation, constitutes our oneness with
all spiritual being and idea, with every spiritual activity, every
spiritual substance, and with every spiritual law.

When we have achieved that oneness with our Source by being grafted back onto the tree through our meditations, we have
become one with everybody on this entire globe and, for all we
know, with influences that may be coming from other planets.
We are not aware of where our good is coming from. We only
know that if we are at-one with God in our meditation, we are
then at-one with the entire universe, and all the good of that
universe is part of our individual experience.

When we are consciously one with God, we become universal: universal in the opportunity to serve and universal in the
sense of being fed and cared for from a universal Source, and
not just from what we see or know about. Thus, every meditation is a uniting with our Source, which in turn unites us with
one another.

When in our class, lecture, or study group meetings we unite
in meditation with our Source, we must remember that there is
only one Source for everyone in that meeting to draw upon, and
therefore, when we are one with our Source, we are one with
each other. That does not mean one only with those who are
physically present. In being consciously one with God and one
with the group with which we are meeting, we are also one with
one another universally, and eventually all those of our own
state of consciousness are led to us or we are led to them. Wherever they may be in time and space, we shall meet them; and
wherever we may be in time or space, they will meet us, and
there will be the mutual opportunity for spiritual sharing.

We may not personally meet all those persons who are of our own state of consciousness, nor will we know those who are benefited by our meditations because, when that oneness with our Source is achieved in our meditation, we do not know who there may be in any part of the world on our own spiritual level who is also tuning in to his Source, and has thus made contact with the state of consciousness which we are. Many times it is reported that someone has been miraculously healed of something or other. There was no apparent reason for his healing: it just happened, and he may never discover why, nor realize that in his extremity he turned within and touched the consciousness of someone, somewhere, also in touch with the Father.

Unfolding Spiritual Experiences

In scriptural and mystical literature, there are accounts of countless men who have attained the mystical state of conscious oneness with God. With the aid of Scripture and with the revelations of mystics, it is possible to embark on a program of individual spiritual living, study, meditation, and practice until we find ourselves experiencing some measure of Christhood. We do not come into our Christhood in a single moment, although we have mystical experiences during which we may experience It in Its fullness. These are momentary experiences, however, after which we come back to earth again and live out from only a tiny measure of spiritual discernment, whereas in memory we have the recollection of the experience in its totality.

As students persist in their study, meditation, and in their seeking of instruction, these spiritual experiences occur more frequently, are of longer duration, and eventually many students enter a phase of consciousness in which the Spirit is upon them, and they are more or less continuously in the Spirit, although not always in the same degree. In other words, they never are

completely out of the Spirit, but on the other hand, only infre-
quently can they live in the full measure of spiritual realization.

Living Through the Spirit

Through the practice of contemplative meditation, we embody
the wisdom of Scripture. This contemplation, or thinking about
truth, however, is not real meditation, but only a step leading up
to the full experience of meditation. The first part of a contemplative meditation is the contemplation of truth, and the second
part is listening for a response from the Father within.

The Spirit of God is already within us, and dwells in us, but it
is of no purpose, nor of any benefit until we become consciously
aware of Its presence. It is exactly as if we had inherited a hundred thousand dollars, but if we have no knowledge of our inheritance the money would be of no use to us. We have it, we own
it, we have title to it, but it is of no value because we do not
know about it. Once we are informed that this hundred thousand
dollars is ours, we accept it and use it, doing what we like with it.
So it is with the Spirit of God. The Spirit of God dwells in us,
but until we know that It does and until we have an awareness of
It, It cannot bear fruit in our experience.

From the moment we have the first conscious experience of
realizing that there is a Presence within us, It will guide us into
the full and complete revelation of truth. If we keep turning to It
within, in the silence, in one way or another It will begin to
make Itself known; It will begin to identify Itself; and once we
have been touched by It, if we keep turning to It faithfully, we
will be led into the fullness of It. "But the Comforter, which is
the Holy Ghost, whom the Father will send in my name, he shall
teach you all things." [1]

Life, after the Spirit of God is upon us, is very different from

[1] John 14:26.

living as a piece of clay in mortality. Our great concern now is not about ourselves, but that this Spirit of God in us will be a benediction to the world and to all who come into our world. Only when this Spirit is in us do we truly live. Life is then lived "not by might, nor by power, but by my spirit." [2]

Father, I am contemplating Thy grace and Thy will so that Thy Spirit may visit me, and so that I may be endowed from on High by Thy Spirit—not by my wisdom, not by my hard work, but by Thy Spirit.

"It is the spirit that quickeneth; the flesh profiteth nothing: the words that I speak unto you, they are spirit, and they are life." [3] When the Spirit of God dwells in us, it is the word of God that is living even our body because it is then not your body or my body: it is God's body. Left to itself, this body can do nothing and go no place. It is the state of consciousness of the individual that governs the entire activity and functioning of the body.

From the human standpoint, we can use the body for good purposes or bad, but when the Spirit of God dwells in us, we can no longer use the body for any purpose. It is no longer our body: it is now the body of God, and it is God who determines what the body shall do, where it shall go, and how it shall be maintained. In other words, the flesh that "profiteth nothing" is "dead": it is "the words that I speak"—God speaks—"they are spirit, and they are life," they are truth and they are power. We have now surrendered control to the Spirit:

Father, this body is Yours, even as I am Yours. I am Your holy temple because You dwell in me. My body is Your temple because I have surrendered it to Your use. Send it where You wish it to be; instruct it to do what You wish it to do.

[2] Zechariah 4:6.
[3] John 6:63.

Receptivity Is Developed
Through Contemplative Meditation

The whole function of contemplative meditation is to bring us to
a point of receptivity where the Father speaks to us. It really
makes no difference whether God speaks in an audible voice,
whether we are just receiving impressions, or whether we are
instinctively doing that which the Spirit forces us to do. The
Spirit makes Itself known in so many different ways that no one
can outline how It will speak to any one person. Eventually,
contemplative meditation brings us to a point of surrender in
which our soul, mind, and body belong to the Spirit of God because the Spirit of God dwells in us.

> *"The Lord will perfect that which concerneth me."* [4] *There is
> no worry and no concern about the things of the outside world
> because the Spirit of God that dwells in me does the work that is
> given me to do. The government is on His shoulders.*

In our contemplation of truth, we reach a place where no
more truth comes, and we seem to have reached the end of our
contemplation. This is the moment when we enter the real meditation. We have thought all we can think about God; we have
said all we can say about God; we have repeated all the prom-
ises; we have brought God's word to conscious remembrance,
and now it is God's turn:

> *Speak, Lord; and I will listen. Speak Thou to me, Lord; make
> Thy will known unto me; make Thy way clear to me; quicken
> Thy Spirit within me; let Thy Spirit bear intercession with my
> Spirit.*

In that humility of Spirit, the silence deepens, and we are a
complete state of receptivity, listening and expectant:

[4] Psalm 138:8.

> *Thy will is done in me. Thy Spirit prospers my way. Thy Spirit feeds, clothes, and houses me; Thy Spirit is my capacity and my ability.*
>
> *It is Thy Spirit that quickeneth and giveth life. The flesh is dead—nothing. Thy Spirit giveth life. "Speak, Lord; for thy servant heareth."* [5]

And so we continue resting in the Spirit for one, two, three, or four minutes, and then we go about our business. If at first we receive no response and nothing seems to happen, that should not disturb us. From the first moment that we engaged in contemplative meditation, something has been happening. It is only a question of when it is going to be made visible in the external.

As we continue this practice, the day does come when that Spirit of the Lord God is upon us, and we consciously feel the presence of God. Each one feels It in a different way for there is no such thing as a particular way in which to identify It. It is enough that we do know that something has happened; we do know that there is now a Presence with us, and even though It does not remain, by returning day after day to our contemplative meditation, we enter the full meditation and receive the word of God which is our life.

A Technique for Transcending the Mind

It is in transcending mind and thought, in the ability to refrain from speech and to achieve and maintain an inner stillness, that the meditative experience is accomplished. This inner stillness is attained when we are able to look at a person, thing, or a condition without labeling it as either good or evil. Then the mind has nothing left to grasp or to think upon; it has nothing to worry about, and it has nothing to rejoice in, or over: it just becomes still.

[5] I Samuel 3:9.

It is like looking at a painting objectively with no preconceived idea as to whether it is good or bad, with no opinion based on the reputation of the artist or on our liking for the subject. Viewing a work of art with that detachment enables us to see the artist's vision: what was in his mind, soul, and consciousness when the painting was made. How much more should we look at spiritual creation, not through our preconceived notions of what human beings should be like, but through the consciousness of the divine Creator!

The only way in which this can be done is to relinquish all labels of good and evil, and when judgment has been completely suspended, we are in the consciousness of the spiritual Creator and are able to behold the universe as God beholds it. We have now entered the mind of God; or conversely, when the mind that is judging and labeling is quiescent, the mind of God has become the active mind of us. But there can be no mind of God functioning in us as long as our mind is forming judgments of good or of evil because while we are seeing persons, things, or conditions as good or evil we are using human standards of judgment, and no human judgment can ever see into the real nature of creation. If we would rightly view this world, we must view it through the eyes, or the consciousness, of God, and that we cannot do until the human mind is still and has relinquished its judgments as to good and evil.

A practice of this kind helps us to refrain from reaction to outer appearances. This is difficult, but when the ability not to react to appearances is achieved—and all serious students sooner or later do reach that point—spiritual healing comes easily and naturally. We will have gone a long way on our spiritual journey if we can see sickness, sin, alcoholism, and all other such appearances and not react to them, not try to heal or change them, but always remember consciously not to judge after appearances:

"Who made me a judge . . . over you?" [6] *No, I do not accept appearances: I accept the truth that the Spirit of God is within*

[6] Luke 12:14.

you, no matter who the "you" is: prisoner in a prison, thief on the street, alcoholic on the corner, or a dying person in a hospital.

We are not to react to appearances: we are to remember that since God is omnipresence, regardless of what appearance we see with our eyes, it is but an appearance, and because it is only an appearance, we are to do nothing about it except to recognize it as such. That is spiritual discernment; that is the ability not to believe what our eyes see and not to judge after appearances.

All spiritual healing work is based on that one point. If, upon receiving a call for help, a practitioner were to sit down and try to heal somebody, he would not be a practitioner for very long. A practitioner of spiritual healing knows nothing about what is called healing. All that constitutes a spiritual healer is an inner discernment that God is individual life, and, therefore, life is immortal, eternal, and indestructible—a spiritual discernment, which consists of not judging after appearances.

Spiritual Discernment Brings Healing

If we judge by appearances, we are always going to behold sin, disease, death, lack, limitation, wars, and restrictions of all kinds, and we will be bound by them because we will be suffering from our own belief about what we are beholding. When the Spirit of the Lord God is upon us, however, we are given the discernment not to judge after appearances. Then, when we are called upon for any kind of help, we are able to sit in contemplation and meditation and realize:

Father, it is Thy Spirit that quickeneth; it is Thy Spirit that reveals truth right where the picture of error is. Let me hear Thy word.

The most difficult part of this Path is coming to the place where we understand that we are not healers or employment agencies, but that our work is purely on the spiritual level, that level of discernment in which, because the Spirit of God is upon us, we know that the crippled man cannot be crippled because God did not cripple him, and God is the only power there is. We know that the blind man cannot be blind because God did not blind him, and there is no other power but God. There cannot be a sin, nor can there be a disease, because God did not create it, and God is the only creator. This, we do not know with our mind.

We cannot know these things with our minds; we cannot even believe them. When we are spiritually ordained and the Spirit of the Lord God is upon us, however, it is possible for us to see that nobody is a human being: everybody is divine, everbody has this spark of the Divine in him, everybody is the child of God. In that understanding, we can look through the appearance, and then those who have turned to us respond, "I feel better; I am better." Our spiritual discernment has seen through the appearance, and what we could never do as a human being, the Spirit of God can do through us.

It may take months and years for the attainment of this realization of the Spirit—not that it will take years for the Spirit to be upon us—but when It does come to us, It will be only a Babe, and we will have to nurse and nurture It. We will have to dwell secretly and sacredly with It within ourselves until by Its fruits others begin to notice that there is something more to us than flesh alone. What is that something more? The Spirit of God that dwells in us.

How Great Is the Drive Within?

The intensity of the drive within us will determine how many hours a day we will give to meditation and spiritual study. Some persons cannot drive themselves to practice scales for more than an hour a day, and others cannot drive themselves to stop in less than seven or eight hours a day. There are some persons, too, who cannot drive themselves to study spiritual principles more than a few minutes or an hour a day. Their mind seeks relaxation, and it cannot hold itself to this particular discipline. Then there are others who cannot let go of it. All that depends on the drive within. This is not a matter of commendation or blame. There are some not fitted for the spiritual path; there are others who have the capacity for touching its fringes, and that is as far as they can go. Then, there are those who are driven and driven until they reach the goal of conscious communion and conscious union with the Source.

From infancy on, whether it is rattles, dolls, automobiles, television, or radio, everything tends to deflect us from our goal. Everything keeps us so busy out here that we do not have time to discover ourselves, and ultimately we lose the capacity to do this. At first, trying to find that inner stillness and inner peace seems to separate us from the rest of the world. It leaves us with a sense of aloneness, and somehow or other, we must be able to survive that stage.

This is not too much different from a man who in his determination to make a million dollars has to cut himself off from all normal relationships while he is driving himself to get that million. He thinks that after he has made his millions he can return to the world and go back to his enjoyment of the human relationships and companionships of his earlier life, but by that time some of his neighbors have made two millions, and so he cannot stop until he has three.

Unless we are willing to separate ourselves from the world and to have periods for the discovery of our Self, we naturally are not going to succeed in attaining our goal of union with God. But like the man with his million, we find that after we attain this union and communion we are not satisfied until we have all there is of it. And so the drive persists to be in communion with God until the complete and perfect experience is attained.

When we have achieved that, we have the capacity to enjoy relationships with every human being anywhere on our spiritual level. We have rare and rich companionships, but these usually come only after sacrificing human companionships and activities until we have arrived at this oneness with the Source, and then discover our oneness with one another.

Every time we meditate, whether or not we feel any direct results from it, we are drawing closer to an actual communion and union with our Source. Let us think of meditation in terms not only of what it will do to our lives, but of the fruitage that it can bring forth for the world. Every time we attain, even for a second, communion with our Source, we are bringing forth food from that Source, not merely food that feeds us, but food that feeds the world. Through our being fed by that Spirit of the Lord God which is upon us, we can feed others because the spiritual fruitage and food that come through are far too much for any one of us. There are always twelve baskets full left over for the world.

The problems of the world can be settled and peace established only in one way—if the world is spiritually fed. Through communing with our Source, we bring forth the food that feeds the world, and then what takes place in our inner communion becomes the good of the world.

ACROSS THE DESK

As I write this, it is January, 1963, and I have just canceled the lecture and class work scheduled up to June 30, so as to remain at home for a longer period of rest and spiritual renewal. The entire basis of our work is that we live out from spiritual consciousness, but a year like 1962 of constant travel, and then coming home to about three thousand pieces of incoming mail, two thousand of which required answers, did not leave much time for the rest and renewal essential to living in that consciousness. Therefore, I will not leave Hawaii until I know that the message that comes forth will spring from the very depths of spiritual consciousness.

The year 1962 saw the world faced with tremendous difficulties and upheavals in North, Central, and South Africa, Southeast Asia, Berlin, and Cuba, to say nothing at all of the problems of finance and industry in the United States. Judging from appearances, the world calls all of this evil, but I say to you that none of this is evil; rather is it all good, and I seriously mean good.

Why do you think the Master said, "I came not to send peace, but a sword"? [7] Do you know how many countries in Africa and Asia have attained their freedom in the past fifteen years, and this because of upheavals, wars, and threats of wars? None of these freedoms would have come about without first having had the upheavals.

Do we not discover, as we enter the spiritual path, that there are also upheavals physically, mentally, and sometimes financially, because our harmony has been based, not on a spiritual foundation, but merely on material law and order? Those who enter the spiritual path cannot forever abide on a material basis or foundation of life because if they do they will experience only physical, material, or financial harmony. And where is the spiritual advancement in this?

Rising to spiritual heights is possible only through what Scripture refers to as "dying daily," but many students on the spiritual path have the idea that if they have some temporary feeling of depression or a mental disturbance, this is "dying daily." Far be it from such. Sometimes we are completely stripped of our health or of our supply, if this be necessary, in order that we may change our foundation from the material sense of good to the spiritual awareness of divine harmony.

For this reason, then, the Master "came not to send peace, but a sword." He came to awaken and arouse us, to pull us out of living on yesterday's manna so that we might rise to the reali-

[7] Matthew 10:34.

zation of spiritual good, spiritual harmony, spiritual freedom, and spiritual peace.

Out of the world's turmoil in the present era will come the freedom of the nations of tomorrow. Of course, it is said that these nations are not yet ready for it, but they never will be ready for it until it comes. Whenever freedom comes, there is always a period of adjustment, preceding and following its attainment, just as there was with the American Colonies after the Revolutionary War before the loosely knit confederation of states was welded together into a nation. Nor was England ready for freedom at the time of the Magna Carta, or even as late as when the Bill of Rights was signed, but each struggle, each upheaval, from the days of the Magna Carta down through and after the Bill of Rights, was a step leading to that freedom which the English people now enjoy under their parliamentary form of government.

No one is ever ready for anything until he experiences it, but the very experiencing of it indicates that the moment of readiness for it has come. Today, the Christ has entered human consciousness through the meditations of those who have prepared the way, and It will overturn, and overturn, and overturn until spiritual harmony and spiritual peace and spiritual prosperity prevail throughout the world.

If we were to judge from appearances, the American Revolution, the wars before and following the Magna Carta of England, the French Revolution, and the South American revolutions were all evil; but who, looking back, would so label them? It is true that all these wars and upheavals would have been unnecessary if—*if, if, if, if*—mankind had only been ready to stop depending on yesterday's manna and been willing to release its hold on what it considered its good so that all the rest of mankind could share in it. But mankind is not made after that pattern: only spiritual man has such capacities.

There would be no need of strikes, such as those that torment the United States and other countries, if men were ready, voluntarily, to share with their brothers, but until such time, the very fact that the worker has the privilege of striking must be looked upon as an instrument for good, even though to our human sense there seems to be so much evil involved in the process.

"Judge not according to the appearance, but judge righteous judgment." [8] Be willing to rest and abide in the truth that the Christ has entered human consciousness, and will overturn until each one comes into the awareness of his spiritual identity and enjoys the fruitage of spiritual living.

[8] John 7:24.

The Power of Resurrection

———•———

History is filled with accounts of man's attempts to find a power that will be stronger than his fears, and with which he can surmount the fears that make of his life one long nightmare. Every nation has sought to free itself from fear by amassing tremendous concentrations of armaments, but what has been the result of this attempt to settle the world's fears by the use of more and more power? The fears remain, and the enemies!

Practically all fears that ever touch an individual, as well as the fears that touch the life of his nation, are related in some way and to some extent to the one word "power": the dreaded power of bombs, the hated power of dictators, or the frightening power inherent in economic cycles. Always there is some power to be feared.

Let us suppose right now that we were to withdraw power from the things or persons that we fear, or suppose that we were to withdraw fear from the powers that we fear. Suppose that for just a single moment we could give up the word "power" in thinking of our personal, national, and international relationships.

To make this concrete, let us bring it down to ourselves and consider what would happen if you and I determined to live in a relationship in which we never used the word "power," never thought of any power that we have over one another, or of using a power to get our way or to enforce our will. Under such a relationship, I would want to live in harmony with you, and you would want to live in harmony with me, but we would no longer have access to any power. In other words, we would have no way of enforcing our will, desire, or hopes. Where would we be then in relationship to one another, with each of us desiring harmony, peace, joy, and friendship, and yet no longer being able to promise or threaten each other? By withdrawing the word "power" from our experience, and all that it implies, it would seem that we have placed ourselves in an absolutely defenseless position.

To continue such philosophic conjecture and speculation does not lead us up a dead-end street, but rather to the realization that the powers that we have been fearing are not really powers, not those that were going to do either such terrible things to us or such wonderful things for us. These powers are not powers at all: they operate as power only in the consciousness that accepts them as power; and for this reason, therefore, any power they may seem to have is only of a temporary nature, and it is a temporary sense of power that causes all our fears. The ultimate of this unfoldment is that power does not exist in that which has form or effect: power is in the consciousness that produces the form or the effect.

Gaining a Release from Fear

The result of a spiritual unfoldment of this nature is to lift the individual above the realm of fear. This release from fear, however, is not achieved instantaneously. There are few of us who can rise immediately to the point of saying, "I do not fear an atomic bomb." We have to begin with things which seem less powerful, perhaps with the weather or climate, with food or germs, and withdraw power from these by understanding that, in and of themselves, they cannot have power because all power is in the consciousness that produces the form, not in the form.

To attain this state of consciousness, it is helpful in our meditation to practice beholding effects, looking out at the weather, the climate, food, germs, and perceiving that they of themselves have no power except the power with which we imbue them. The power is within our consciousness. Shakespeare expressed it succinctly when he said, "There is nothing either good or bad, but thinking makes it so."[1] In other words, the evil is not in the thing, nor is it in the effect. Whatever evil there is, is in our sense of what we are beholding, or in the power with which we imbue an individual, a condition, or a circumstance.

Most of us have already demonstrated this in some degree, and have proved that many of the so-called powers of the world have been rendered powerless by our spiritual awareness. We have experienced, some in small degree and some in very great degree, the operation of this principle in our life, but until we consciously take it into our Self, into our inner sanctuary, and abide in it, we cannot make it practical in our daily experience. True, we can receive benefit from those who have attained the consciousness of nonpower, but this is of only temporary help to us.

Eventually we must take this subject into meditation, let our

[1] *Hamlet.* Act II.

thought wander across the whole span of our human life, and make a mental check of those things, persons, or conditions we have feared, and begin to silence those fears by withdrawing power from things, persons, or conditions, realizing:

> *God is infinite consciousness, the consciousness of the entire universe. It is out of that Consciousness, which is God, that the whole world has become manifest. God looked upon His universe and saw that it was all good. God, as Consciousness, the Substance of the entire spiritual creation, could create and manifest a world only in the image and likeness of Himself. Therefore, this spiritual universe is imbued with the qualities of God, and with no other qualities. Only God entered His own universe—only the qualities and the activities of God—and therefore, all that exists is in and of God.*

There is no evil power in the spiritual creation because there is no evil power in God. "In him is no darkness at all." [2] Nothing could ever enter the consciousness of God "that defileth . . . or maketh a lie." [3] God is too pure to behold iniquity. The consciousness of God is absolute purity, life eternal, immortality itself.

Life Is the Eternal Reality

"For I have no pleasure in the death of him that dieth . . . wherefore turn yourselves, and live ye." [4] God has not created death or anything that could cause death. God is pure, undefiled Spirit, life eternal; and God, functioning as the consciousness of Christ Jesus, says, "I am come that they might have life, and that they might have it more abundantly" [5]—not "I have come that they might have death," or not "I have come that they

[2] I John 1:5.
[3] Revelation 21:27.
[4] Ezekiel 18:32.
[5] John 10:10.

might have life until they are threescore years and ten," but "I am come that they might have life more abundantly." Furthermore, the voice of God, again speaking as the consciousness of Christ Jesus, says, "I am the resurrection, and the life." [6] Always God is voicing the eternality and immortality of man. Nothing was ever created by God that is empowered to cause the distress of man. There is no room in the life more abundant for death or for anything that would cause death.

As we go back into the original spiritual creation as revealed in the first chapter of Genesis, there is not one single sign of discord or of anything that has power to destroy God's universe. If there were, we would be admitting that God, the Creator, is also God, the Destroyer; that God at the time of creation also made something to destroy His own creation. There is only one sense in which the Oriental teaching of God as both Creator and Destroyer can be accepted, and that is that God as Creator of the universe must automatically be the destroyer of anything that is contrary to the spiritual creation. That, however, would never mean the destroyer of anything real.

Since God is the Self-created, Self-maintaining, Self-sustaining principle of this universe, the responsibility for our immortality and eternality rests with God, not with man, not with bombs, not with germs, and not with the upswings or downswings of Wall Street. The fate of man is not in effect, but in Consciousness, the Consciousness which is God, the infinite, the divine, the pure. Actually, this Consciousness is the consciousness of man, and in its unconditioned state leaves man, as it did Melchizedek, spiritual, untouched by mortal conditions, material circumstances, or human beliefs.

[6] John 11:25.

Attaining the Unconditioned Consciousness

The evils that befall us are not in God or in man, but rather in the conditioning that we have received through the ignorance that has been foisted upon us from time immemorial. In other words, every time that we give power to a person, a thing, or a condition, our consciousness is showing forth its conditioning, and to that extent we become victims of it.

It might come as a surprise to see how easy it would be for some person, either for a specific purpose or just as an experiment, to show us how quickly we could be made to distrust one another, and then in the end, fear one another. It has been done over, and over, and over again. It is a very simple thing to condition the minds of persons who are not alert so that they unthinkingly accept the opinions, thoughts, and beliefs of others and respond robotlike to individual suggestion or mass hysteria. If we listened to all the propaganda and the opinions of others, very soon we would be fighting not only with our families, but with our neighbors and the whole world.

The question is this: To whom do we give allegiance? To whom do we surrender our minds and our thoughts? It is very difficult for persons who have not been taught the value of meditation to turn within to the Presence for Its guidance, instruction, and wisdom. Instead, they rely on opinions gathered from newspapers, magazines, television broadcasts, and thereby fear every headline, as if it could be a threat to the life which is God.

If it is true that the kingdom of God is within us, then the kingdom of power is within us because God is power, and not only is God power, but God is all the power there is. God is omnipotence. If we can accept God as All-power, and if we can accept the presence of God, the power of God, and the kingdom of God as being within us, then we can understand that the place

whereon we stand is holy ground. Why? Because we are inseparable and indivisible from our Father, for the kingdom of our
Father is within us. The kingdom of Omnipotence is within us,
but only as we meditate upon this can we look out and state with
conviction: "I will not fear what mortal man or mortal conditions can do to me. I will not fear what mortality can do; I will
not fear what germs or bombs can do because the kingdom of
God, Omnipotence, is within me. All-power is within me."

Ordinarily, God is accepted, not as Omnipotence, but merely
as a great Power to be invoked over whatever the enemy may
seem to be. It could be sin, disease, or death; it could be war; it
could be anything. Regardless of all our prayers for health,
safety, and peace, these are still absent from the world. And
why? Have not our prayers been unsuccessful because God is
not a great power over lesser powers? God is omnipotence, and
these other powers are not powers, except in proportion as we
are conditioned to accept them.

One has only to travel the world to witness the fears that are
hammering at the consciousness of men. Is there any hope for
freedom in the world until there is a release from fear? Is not
fear at the root of all problems: personal, national, and international? Is not fear the real bugaboo?

Holdups have been committed with toy pistols even though
there is no power in a toy. Was not the power in the acceptance
of it as a real weapon? How many persons have died through the
diabolic suggestions of the kahunas of ancient times! How many
persons have been made miserable through witchcraft! Was there
ever any real power in kahunas or in witches or witchcraft? Was
not the power in the fear that these were a power, a fear that took
possession of the victim?

Recently, experiments have been conducted whereby one half
of a group of persons were fed cold germs, and the other half
capsules of water. They all believed that they were being given
cold germs, and about the same percentage in each group caught
cold; but when the procedure was reversed, the same results

were obtained. The power was not in the capsules: it was the minds of those participating in the experiment that gave the capsules the only power they had.

In our unconditioned state, we are immortal and eternal, and nothing external to us and nobody external to us have power, jurisdiction, or control over us. We are individuals, yet one with God. All the Omnipotence, all the divine Grace, all the divine Love, all the divine Power are ours. Therefore, nothing external to us can act upon us.

If we permit ourselves to be conditioned through an acceptance of universal beliefs and universal fears, however, then they act upon us in the same way as they act upon the rest of the human race, and we make ourselves victims of them. We do not fear ghosts, but there are some persons who do. Is there any power in ghosts, or is the power in the fear of them?

There are today perhaps millions of persons in the world virtually untouched by harmful germs and practically immune to germ-diseases. Why? Is this because there are fewer germs in their systems than in anybody else's? Or is it because they have accepted Omnipotence, because they have agreed that all the power of God is given unto them, not unto germs, weather, or climate? God has endowed every one of us with His power; God has given us dominion over all that exists on the earth, under the earth, and above the earth. This dominion we have surrendered by permitting ourselves to be conditioned by the world's ignorance and the world's fears.

Resurrection Here and Now

In our oneness with the Father, we find not only spiritual power but food, water, inspiration, and even resurrection. How often we hear the questions: "Do you believe in resurrection? Did Jesus rise from a tomb? Did anyone see the risen Jesus? Did he walk the earth?"

Those who do not believe that Jesus was crucified and entombed, that he rose from the tomb and walked the earth, do not
have the spiritual vision that would enable them to see that
which the eyes cannot see, and hear that which the ears cannot
hear. The truth is that Jesus was crucified; he was entombed; he
rose from the tomb; he walked the earth, and was seen by at
least five hundred persons who bore witness to that fact.

This was the truth about Jesus beyond all question of doubt,
but this is also the truth about all of us. We, too, will walk freely
on the earth after our so-called burial. The only difference is that
there will not be five hundred persons to identify us because we
have not told them to expect us or to believe in our powers of
resurrection. So our friends will turn away from our funeral with
grief, believing we have gone somewhere, and according to their
belief so will it be unto them.

The dead are never entombed in the grave, and they are never
cremated. That happens only to the shell, the body. I know this
to be true because I have actually seen those who have passed
away standing in my presence, and in some cases have heard
them speaking to me.

Each of us, in his time, will pass from visible sight, and this is
in accord with divine Wisdom, which enables us to outgrow the
form of an infant and become a child, then to outgrow the form
of a child to become a mature person, and to continue maturing
until we have outgrown the need for this particular form or
body, and are enabled to make a transition so that we may function in still another form.

If everyone remained on this earth forever, there would be
no opportunity for the coming generations, nor would there be
any activity for the older citizens who have outgrown their ability to serve the world. Provision must, therefore, be made for
continued growth and unfoldment, and after a certain length of
time on this earth, these cannot come to us here.

I am sure that there are many who make the transition before
their time, many who are forced out by disease or poverty, and

this will change only as the world becomes more spiritually minded. But when we see those of mature years go forward to a new experience, we should rejoice in the greater opportunity that is now being given them to function usefully, harmoniously, and joyously.

It is destined that we be immortal, for the offspring of God cannot be less immortal than God. We are immortal, temporarily clothed upon with a belief that we are mortal. We are clothed upon with mortality, but the Christ-message is that we must be unclothed; we must remove from ourselves this false concept of self, which claims that we are mortal, and we must be clothed upon with immortality. We must "die daily" to our mortality and be reborn into our immortality.

From beginning to end, Scripture reveals that there is a power that restores to us "the years that the locust hath eaten." [7] There is a power of resurrection, a power of restoration, regeneration, and renewal, and it is this power within us that the Master came to reveal. He restored to full and complete dignity the woman taken in adultery; he restored to heaven the thief on the cross. What was that restoration and regeneration but a resurrection?

Love Is the Power of Resurrection

The power of resurrection lies in love, but it is difficult to understand what love is. Everybody wants to be loved, but so few want to love, and it is only in loving that resurrection can come, not in being loved. We could be loved by millions, and still die miserably. The power of resurrection is not in the love that is given to us: the power of resurrection is in the love that flows through us and out from us. In other words, the "imprisoned splendor" must be permitted to escape, and that imprisoned

7 Joel 2:25.

splendor is our life eternal. But life is love, and there is no life separate and apart from love.

So many persons find life to be futile, not really worthwhile, and when we come to know them, we see why. The power of loving has left them—not the power of being loved. They spend most of their life seeking for companionship and understanding, which they never quite succeed in finding because they are not to be found: they are to be expressed.

If we want life—and I mean life harmonious, not just an existence from morning to night, and night to morning; real life, a life abundant in every way, physically, mentally, morally, financially—we do not go around looking for life: we live, we live! A man who had attained a hundred years and was asked how he had reached such an advanced age wisely answered, "I just kept on living." Of course that was the answer, but we cannot just keep on living unless we have something to live for. The moment a reason for living disappears, life disappears.

The only reason there is for living is to love. It sounds strange, but it is true. There is no other reason for staying on earth than the opportunity to love, and anybody who has experienced this knows that there is no joy like loving: no joy like sharing, bestowing, understanding, and giving, all of which are but other names for love.

It is difficult to make this clear to those who are living entirely from the standpoint of getting, wanting, and desiring. On the other hand, it is simple to explain this to a person who has within himself some touch of the Spirit of God. Unfortunately, there are some devoid of this Spirit of God; and these, the Master referred to as barren and rocky soil. One thing is missing in them, one thing only: love, love. The love they are seeking is the love they must give. Once that love is there, once that nature that wants to give, share, and understand is there, the nature that wants to meet this world halfway, the next step is easy: it is gaining the understanding that the real power of this world is in consciousness, not something external to it.

This is our great lesson: God is the infinite, divine consciousness, the consciousness of which this universe is formed, and God has given Himself to us so that the life and consciousness of God may be ours. The whole, immortal life of God is ours; the whole divine consciousness of God is ours—all this divine Consciousness.

Learning to Release the Gift of God

Since we are already infinite, there is no need for us to seek good, love, companionship, or supply: we are already one with the Father, and all that the Father has is already ours. In order to enjoy our spiritual heritage, we must learn how to let this gift of God escape.

One way of doing this is by living constantly in the awareness that dominion has been given to us—God-dominion, spiritual dominion—and therefore we need not fear anything or anyone external to ourselves. The second way is to open up ways for a greater expression of love to flow out from us. The Master has pointed out how this love can be expressed: we can visit the prisoner in prison; we can comfort the widow and the orphan; we can heal the sick; we can feed the hungry; we can clothe the naked; we can pray; we can pray for our enemies; we can forgive seventy times seven. All this is loving, all this is letting love flow out.

In one way or another, we must ask ourselves the question, "What have I in my house?" The moment we say, "I," that brings us right back to "I and my Father are one." [8] All that the Father has is ours to share: all the love, all the life, all the dominion, all the Grace, all the supply. Even if we only share the few drops of oil that may be immediately available, or the little meal, or if we begin with that old pair of shoes in the closet—no

[8] John 10:30.

matter where we begin—if we begin to pour out what we have in the house, it increases, and the more it is used, the more it increases.

It is like teaching. No student has ever learned as much from a teacher as the teacher learns from teaching the student because it is in the teaching that the flow begins, and the more the teacher pours out, the more is pouring in. Whether it is teaching on the spiritual level or on the human level, the more experience or practice a teacher has in his particular field, the greater his own knowledge becomes because the flow is from the infinite Source that is within each one of us. Infinity is within us; the kingdom of God is within us; and we draw from this infinite source of Withinness the moment we acknowledge, "I and my Father are one."

All Power Is Within Us

As we seat ourselves comfortably for our meditation, with our eyes closed, we are looking into darkness, and we can see the infinite nature of this darkness which is our Withinness, full and complete. All this darkness is within us, all this space is within us, all this world that we are confronting is within us:

> Now, here where I am, within me, within this very darkness, is the kingdom of God. The kingdom of Allness, of Omnipotence, of divine Grace is stored up here within me.

If we were sitting alone in a rubber boat in the middle of the ocean, this realization would bring us protection, safety, food, water, or whatever we needed. If we were lost in the desert, this realization would lead us, even with our eyes closed, out of the desert into safety and security, or would lead others to us, since right where we are, God is: the fullness of God, the allness of God, the omnipotence of God, the grace of God.

When we know this, we have no fear of any circumstance or condition in the outer world because all dominion is within us. A thousand of those who do not know this truth may fall at our left hand, and ten thousand at our right, but it will not come nigh our dwelling place. As we realize the very presence of this Omnipotence within us, God is abiding in us, and we bear fruit richly.

Through practicing this one principle of the nature of spiritual power, we are living the Christ-life. The Master feared no disease, no death; he feared no Pilate. "Thou couldest have no power at all against me, except it were given thee from above." [9] Pilate is only another name for the particular tyrant seeming to operate in our experience.

Because of his realization of Omnipotence, Jesus feared nothing external to him; but at the same time he was not fearing external powers, he was pouring forth to the world his love, his healing consciousness, his sharing consciousness, his forgiving consciousness, and not only pouring it forth to the saints but to the sinners as well.

We must do likewise that we may be disciples, that we may be the sons of God. We are not fulfilling ourselves as children of God unless, first of all, we are acknowledging Omnipotence within ourselves, and thereby fearing nothing external, and secondly, letting the Christ-love pour fourth in infinite abundance. Then we shall witness the resurrection taking place within us here and now.

ACROSS THE DESK

Consciousness is the most important word in the entire vocabulary of The Infinite Way. Nothing we can think of can ever take the place of the word "Consciousness." In Its pure state, Consciousness is God; and in Its pure state, It constitutes our being. As human beings, we live as states and stages of consciousness,

[9] John 19:11.

degrees of consciousness. In fact, the moment we are conceived humanly, the consciousness we are begins to receive conditioning. We are conditioned by all that our parents think: the fears and the hopes they entertain are transferred to us. Then we enter school and are conditioned by schoolteachers, schoolmates, and parents of schoolmates, always picking up more conditioning so that by the time we go out into the world 90 per cent of the things we are convinced are true are in reality untrue. Out in the world on our own, the conditioning continues.

From the moment we touch a metaphysical teaching, however, we begin to condition ourselves along other lines. For example, if we pondered the statement, "Call no man your father upon the earth: for one is your Father, which is in heaven," [10] and if the truth of that principle ever registered in our consciousness, we would soon be able to look around and say, "Oh, then there is only one Creator, and we are all children of that One; we are all equal in the sight of God."

That alone would wipe out of us our prejudices and early conditioning toward other persons. On this point, we would have a new consciousness. We would have "died" to the state of consciousness which had been filled with biases and prejudices and we would have become one with our fellow man universally. On this one point, we would have become a new man.

If this kind of conditioning continued, eventually we would come to another extension of that same idea and would realize that if this is true, we then derive our qualities and inheritances from that One. It was Emerson who said, "There is but one universal Mind, and all men are inlets to, and outlets from, that One." Once we begin to perceive that we are inlets to and outlets from that one God-consciousness, we perceive that we are inlets to and outlets for Its qualities, and we are not limited as we thought we were; we are not dependent on what our human parents were: now we are dependent on our Source. It might

[10] Matthew 23:9.

take months of pondering, but eventually it would sink in, and we could then say that whereas we were blind, now we see.

Through a realization of this one truth, we begin to draw on Infinity; we are in a new consciousness in which two things have happened: we have lost our bias and our bigotry and have thrown off some of the handicaps and limitations of our ancestors. No longer is it true that the sins of the fathers shall be visited "upon the children unto the third and fourth generation." [11] Once we take this one principle and work with it, we are a freer state of consciousness; we are not the same person; we have thrown off our dependency on others and have learned to go within to the Source.

Every one of us from childhood has been told to fear external powers, whether in the form of germs, infection, contagion, or weather. But what if we were to catch a glimpse of the metaphysical principle, "Pilate, you have no power over me. 'I and my Father are one.' God gave me dominion, and because of that dominion, there is no power in the external world"? Would not the acceptance of this principle and the conviction of its truth set us free from 70 to 80 per cent of the world's fears? We would no longer fear the power of anything external to us, and again on this one point, we would be a different state of consciousness: we would have "died" to our fears.

We have not yet "died" to the greatest fear of all, the fear of death. It is this fear that makes illnesses so frightening. If there is such a thing as becoming immune to the fear of death, then we would have demonstrated living eternally, and I do not mean by that staying on earth forever.

We all will have to make a transition, but the time for that transition is when we have served our purpose on earth, and while we might look forward to the transition, we no longer look forward to death. In losing the fear of death, we are set free from most of the diseases of this world, and with even a partial

[11] Exodus 20:5.

movement into that state, we are not the same person we were before. No longer are we fearing outer conditions and circumstances. We have moved into still another degree of consciousness.

By this time in our spiritual life, we are in a state of consciousness entirely different from what we were the day we found ourselves on the spiritual path. We are no longer giving power to the external; we have fewer superstitious beliefs; and we have lost some of our ignorance. This progress is made only as we take one spiritual principle after another and work with it until each one "rings a bell" and registers within.

As consciousness is purified, that is, as we rid ourselves of erroneous conditioning, more and more do we approach the pure Consciousness, God-given life and immortality. Now, as always, our prayer should be, "Father, give me the pure Consciousness I had with Thee before the world began."

The basic principle emphasized in The Infinite Way is that there is neither good nor evil but thinking makes it so. We neither look to external good nor fear external evil. Nothing—no thing—has been empowered with evil. God has given us His own Spirit, His own consciousness. The degree of our failure can be measured by the degree to which we have picked up man's universal consciousness.

Each one has within himself his own degree of realization of that mind which was also in Christ Jesus. When we consciously know the truth, we are attaining that mind. In proportion as we give no power to the external, we will understand that eventually the lamb will lie down with the lion, and as we adopt this principle in our life, we will find that we are affected less and less by the external. The closer we come to the principle, the closer we come to a consciousness of good.

This becomes more and more true as our consciousness can accept the revelation that there is neither good nor evil, that it is only the universal sense that makes it seem so. There is just *IS*. The grass *IS,* the weather *IS,* the water *IS*. The only power there is, is Being. The closer we live to the consciousness that all is Being, God created and God endowed, the more we find ourselves attuned to the love of God and the grace of God. This then changes our consciousness because a life free of some of the old fears is a whole new consciousness.

Every time we receive an inner impartation, it knocks out some external fear, and to a degree we are freed from our early outside conditioning. If we could look back ten years and see ourselves as we were then, we would say, "Why, I am not that person."

The reason the word "consciousness" is so important is because we know that the goal of our work is to change our consciousness. In accomplishing this, we have to leave the world alone. Any change that takes place has to come from within our own consciousness. Let us ask ourselves: What is our reaction to persons, weather, theories? What is our reaction to death? We do not know what special conditioning of mind is our particular barrier, and it is because we do not know what is limiting us that we need frequent periods of meditation.

Eventually, we come into an awareness that our consciousness determines the nature of our life, but it is only as we accept a change of consciousness that the change can come. No teacher or practitioner brings about a change in a student: he is only the instrument through which the student himself makes the change. The thing to be grateful for is the inner God that prepared us for the change. Whatever degree of changed consciousness comes to us depends upon our devotion to that end. A teacher or practitioner is only the means to the end. He has the power to bring out what is in us and no more, and that only in proportion to our humility and willingness to pitch in and work.

There is something inside that is pushing us toward attaining a pure consciousness. Somewhere in a past incarnation or in the present one, something happened to spark our spiritual center, and as each one of these specific principles becomes illumined in us, we get closer to the pure state of consciousness. Then as we make each of the principles our own, we have taken one step out of human bondage, and we are tied less to human limitation.

In proportion to our ability to grasp and become convinced of the truth that there is neither good nor evil, we become pure Consciousness. Pure Consciousness is that of which we are composed: the states of consciousness we express are superimposed by the beliefs of the world. To attain pure Consciousness involves a process of "dying daily." Every time we drop a theory, every time we drop an anxiety or a superstition, to that extent we have "died" to this world.

When the Master said that he had overcome the world, he had overcome these temptations, but when he had overcome death he had really overcome the world. Personally, I do not think he overcame the world until he was in the Garden of Gethsemane. There he faced death. There he left his human sense of life. No one fully "dies" until he faces death; then he is in the Fourth Dimension. He is then alive not in the human sense but in the spiritual sense.

FIVE

God-Endowed Dominion

The healing principles of The Infinite Way differ so radically from those found in other teachings that students who want to be successful in the practice of Infinite Way healing should work only from the standpoint of what has been given to them in this work.

There are some teachings in which the practitioner endeavors to find the error that is causing the trouble and identify it with the patient. This practice is called "uncovering the error," and assumes that there is some erroneous thought in the patient, which is producing his particular disease.

Early in my practice I discovered that this was not true. Evil does not originate in the patient's thought, although he may permit himself to become an outlet for it. All evil of any nature, whether it is sin, false appetite, disease, lack, or limitation, has its origin in the universal or carnal mind. The moment a practitioner knows this, he begins to set his patient free. Instead of pinning some error on to him and fastening it to him, he immediately realizes, "This does not have its origin in a person: it has its origin in the universal or carnal mind."

Recognize the God in Everyone

If I sit on a class or lecture platform in front of an audience, thinking that everyone in that group is the child of God with the mind of God and the Soul of God and that only God lives and works in and through him, what happens? Even though the members of the class or audience do not know that this silent realization of their true spiritual nature and origin is going on, they begin to respond to the truth about them. They do not know why, but they rejoice inwardly because I am seeing them as they are in their real nature, seeing their real Self, seeing behind the human masquerade.

If, on the other hand, I were to sit on that platform and criticize the persons in the audience, resent or judge them after human standards, they would begin to twist and squirm and feel uncomfortable. Why? Because I would be malpracticing them, and even though they did not know what I was doing, they would feel the effect of it.

This same thing happens in the healing practice. If I try to find the error in a patient, he begins to feel my malpractice, and instead of being free and happy and joyous, he is uncomfortable under my censure and judgment. That is no way to set anyone free.

It is possible to experiment with this principle in dealing with cats, dogs, birds, or little children. Instead of saying, "You bad dog," "You naughty cat," or, "You impudent child," we should realize: "God made individual being, and that being possesses all the qualities of God. The mind and the intelligence of individual being spring from God. Life is of God, and God governs even the sparrow's fall." When this is known, the animal's or the child's behavior changes because condemnation has been removed.

If you would heal, you must remember to remove the original sin from mankind, the belief that man was created in sin and brought forth in iniquity. That is not the truth about anybody. "Call no man your father upon the earth: for one is your Father, which is in heaven." [1] And what does this mean except that you are to recognize the spiritual origin of every man?

Although scientists may trace man back to a seed, the question remains: Where did the seed originate? Was not the seed created by God? Man is not a creator: God is the creator. Man is only the instrument through which creation appears, but behind man is God that created the seed. Everything that is visible, everything that is made, is made of a substance that is invisible.

The Universal Impersonal Nature of Evil

The minute I recognize that God constitutes individual being, I must also recognize that no person contains within himself the source of any evil. There is no evil in anyone, no God-constituted evil and no self-created evil. Any evil that is manifesting through a person has its origin in what for lack of a better name may be called the universal carnal mind. To so dispose of it immediately separates it from the person, and leaves him as he originally was, the image and likeness of God, God Himself in expression, Life expressing Itself as individual being. There is then no evil in him: the only evil there is, is the impersonal evil inherent in the universal carnal mind.

Whenever there is an outbreak of colds, influenza, or other diseases of that nature, there is the belief that weather, climate,

[1] Matthew 23:9.

or germs are the cause, but can you not see that this belief did not originate in the person? He did not originate the idea of colds or flu; he did not originate the idea of germs. This is some kind of a belief out in the atmosphere, which he has picked up because of his ignorance of the truth.

In working with such cases, there is no point in treating a person, because the average practitioner might have a hundred persons with colds or the flu calling for help, and he would have a hard time trying to give each one of them a treatment every day. Fortunately, this is not necessary because there is only one problem, and that problem has nothing to do with a person. It is a universal belief of weather, infection, contagion, or of germs, and when it is handled in this way, if there are a hundred sick, a hundred are healed as each one brings himself to, and touches, the consciousness of the practitioner. Yet there has been only one treatment because there is only one belief: a universal belief in a selfhood apart from God, a power apart from God, or a presence apart from God.

When you experiment with this principle and prove conclusively to yourself that a cold, flu, or pneumonia is not caused by a person's erroneous thinking, you will then be able to apply this principle to other diseases, to sin, and to false appetites. In each case, you will observe that the origin of the problem is not in the person and that you cannot uncover the error in him because it is not there.

The error is in a universal belief that there is a mortal man or that there is a condition or a creation apart from God. It is a *universal* belief, not your belief and not my belief. In The Infinite Way, this is called "impersonalization," and this principle is of primary importance in Infinite Way healing. No matter what the problem is, from corns to cancers, from an empty pocketbook to an empty relationship, it is not a person, and it is not in a person: it is a universal belief of a selfhood and a power apart from God. It is not the person because the person is God made manifest: he is Life expressed; he is Spirit revealed; he is the

Soul of God incarnate. The very breath he breathes is the breath of God. He is really God-Selfhood. There is no evil in him, and there is no sin.

Was it not at the trial of Jesus that Pilate said, "I find in him no fault at all"? [2] That is exactly what our practitioners must say to every case, "I find no fault in this patient, no fault at all, no evil. I find only that he is the Holy One of Israel, the child of God, the offspring of Spirit, the very life of God expressed." This is impersonalizing the appearance.

"Nothingizing" the Problem

After the error has been impersonalized, there is a second step, and this is called "nothingizing," making nothing of it, in other words, realizing that God did not create the evil condition:

> Thou art of purer eyes than to behold evil, and canst not look on iniquity. Habakkuk 1:13

> For I have no pleasure in the death of him that dieth . . . wherefore turn yourselves, and live ye. Ezekiel 18:32

The Master said, "I came down from heaven, not to do mine own will, but the will of him that sent me." [3] The will of the Father is that we be healed of disease, that we be freed of lack, that we be forgiven our sins. Can these errors, then, be of God, and if they are not of God, do they have any power? If they are not of God, can they have any real existence? "And God saw every thing that he had made, and, behold, it was very good." [4] He found no evil in His creation.

This brings us to something you already know, but which you may not have accepted as an absolute principle. You may have

[2] John 18:38.
[3] John 6:38.
[4] Genesis 1:31.

declared that God is the only power, but have you accepted this truth as an absolute principle, or do you continue to accept two powers, a good power and a power of evil? Do you look upon germs as an evil power? Do you look upon dictators as evil men? Do you look upon disease and sin as evil conditions? If you do, you are not accepting God as Omnipotence.

If you would practice spiritual healing, you must accept God as Omnipotence and you must be able to look at sin, false appetite, disease, or any other condition without fear or horror, realizing: "If you are not a part of the omnipotence of God, you can exist only in man's belief." A person can believe that there are ghosts in a room, but the ghosts do not have reality.

You cannot say that evil does not exist as a belief in the mind of men: it does, or else there would be no need for a teaching based on the nonpower of evil because you would not be experiencing any evil. You experience evil only because there is a universal belief in its reality and power. In proportion as you can accept God as Omnipotence does evil lose its seeming power, its power in belief.

There Is No Law of Disease

Some years ago, a physician came to me with a presumably incurable disease. Now, one cannot very well explain the nothingness of disease or its unreal nature to a doctor because he is devoting his life to trying to cure disease. Nevertheless, I could say to him, "This disease has no law to support it. If it had a law, you could not cure it because you cannot break a law. You cannot break the law of two times two is four; you cannot break the law that H_2O is water; you cannot break anything that has a law. And so if a disease had a law to support it, it would be an eternal disease because it would be perpetuated by its law.

"If disease had a law, would not that law have come from

God? Is not God the one and only law-giver? If disease had a law of God governing it, could anybody stop the disease? Or can disease be healed only because it has no law of God to support it?"

Because in his own mind this physician was able to accept the truth that if anything has a law, it has immortality, he had a very beautiful healing.

If you can grasp the principle that disease has no law, it will fall by the very fact that you have recognized its nothingness. If you can comprehend and really understand this truth, the appearance will be dissolved. If you can recognize the truth that God is not responsible for disease and death, you will destroy them both. This is the truth that makes you free.

One Power

Every time you realize the spiritual nature of any person and the universal nature of human beliefs, you are helping to free him from disease, sin, fear, or lack. All these have their basis in the belief of original sin as related in the Bible in the allegory of Adam and Eve. They ate of the tree of the knowledge of good and evil, and it was their acceptance of these two powers that sent them out of the Garden of Eden. Ever since that time, we too have been eating of that tree, thereby keeping ourselves out of Eden.

But we can return to Eden the instant that we realize that God never created two powers. God is the only power, and besides God, there is no other power. Because God is Spirit, the only power there is, is spiritual power, and nothing else is power. Material power is not power; mental power is not power: only Spirit is power.

As you cling to this: "I acknowledge only God as Spirit, God as Law, God as Power; and all else I recognize to be a universal belief of the carnal mind," you find yourself healing because you are not fighting a belief of disease, sin, or lack any more than you would fight the belief that two times two is five. Once you have recognized and realized that evil is not personal, that it has nothing to do with the person who is suffering from it except that temporarily he has accepted it, but otherwise it does not have its rise or origin in him and is no part of his nature, you have won a victory over the error, regardless of what its name or what its nature may be.

Remove Malpractice by Impersonalizing the Error

You must be firm in impersonalizing error. In one breath, you cannot lay the blame for evil at a person's door, and then in the next breath call evil impersonal. You must be absolutely universal in accepting this principle. At first, this is hard to do because there are many persons you might feel are to blame for some of your troubles. I am sure you all believe someone else has caused trouble for you when he really did not. The truth of the matter is that the trouble arose out of your acceptance of the universal belief which made you see the other person as less than the child of God. In that failure, you malpracticed him, and the malpractice came back upon you.

It is literally true that you must call no man on earth your father because you have a spiritual origin. You are the spiritual manifestation of the divine Spirit, the eternal and immortal expression of God Itself. You are not physical; you are not mortal; you are not material; you are really not even human: you are divine. The only part of you that even seems to be mortal arises out of the belief that there are two powers.

When you accept one power, it is easy to understand why the Master did not react to the appearance of disease and sin. He just looked at them and said, "Neither do I condemn thee.[5] . . . Today shalt thou be with me in paradise." [6] In other words, as you reach out to the Christ, recognizing that sin and disease do not have their origin in a person and that he is not responsible for them, he is absolved.

This takes the burden of malpractice off your patient, your student, and off your neighbor. It takes the burden of malpractice away from everybody, even your pets. You do not ask your pets to be spiritual, to read so many pages of so many books, to be more loving, more generous, more kind, or more patient. When your cat, your dog, or your bird is suffering, you know the truth of God as Life, as the only Power and the only Presence. You know that none of these evils belongs to the cat or the dog, that they are just part of a universal mortal belief, and thus you free it. That is the same way you should act toward your patient.

Teaching is quite a different thing. In teaching, students are given instruction and directed to books and to passages in books which will further enlighten them. All the Writings present specific principles for students to learn. This is not so that they may be healed: this is that they may learn the principles which transform consciousness from a material to a spiritual basis.

When someone asks you for help, this must be your response: "Of course, I will give you help at once." It is not necessary to know the nature of the problem or the name of the person who is seeking healing. Nobody has ever told me the names of the cats and dogs for whom help was asked, and yet they were healed without my knowing their names. I have learned that nobody has to tell me the name of the patient who wants to be healed because, as far as I am concerned, he is the same spiritual offspring of God that I am.

What difference whether a flower is called a rose, an orchid, or a violet? It is still a flower. And so, whether a person is called

[5] John 8:11.
[6] Luke 23:43.

Bill, Jim, or Henry, he is still the spiritual offspring of God. I am not transferring any truth to his mind, nor am I communicating any truth to him. I am knowing the truth within me, and the only truth there is about him, or about any "him" it happens to be, is the truth about God. I do not specifically have to know the truth about Mary Jones or Bill Smith: I know the truth about God. I do not believe that God knows the names of those who ask for help any more than I do.

When a problem is presented to you, first of all, you must realize that this is not only not of man, but that it has no real existence: it exists only as an illusory appearance. Look at the difference between a condition and an illusory appearance: a condition, you have to fight; an illusory appearance, you dismiss. If you were treating conditions, you would have to study for years, be licensed, and be a part of the practice of *materia medica*. But you are not treating conditions; you are not treating disease; you are not treating diseased people: you are knowing the truth of man's identity and of the illusory nature of the appearance, thereby dismissing the problem.

You, yourself, however, must be firmly grounded in these principles. You cannot waver between hope one minute, faith the next minute, and doubt another minute. It is for this reason that it is always better to begin the practice of healing with the lesser claims of the human world and build a consciousness of the nonpower of any appearance, although this is not necessary. You can begin with any problem that touches your consciousness if you have learned to impersonalize and to realize instantly that this has nothing to do with a person: this is an impersonal belief in two powers, the Adamic belief, a universal error. In this way, you have taken it away from your patient and immediately placed it where it belongs, as a part of the vast mental illusion. It is an illusory appearance, a false belief of the universal carnal mind.

The Immortality and Eternality of Life

When you have thus separated error from a person, ask your-self: "Is it of God? Did God create this?" No, God could not have created it because God could never have created anything destructive to Himself. Your life is God's life. If anything is happening to your life, it is happening to God's life. Certainly, God who is infinite wisdom and divine love has never made any provision for destroying His own life, and His life is the only life you will ever have. This is why you can know beyond all question that you are immortal: you did not begin on the day that is called your birthday, and your life will not come to an end on the day that is called your death-day. The only life that you live is God's life. It is not really you living: it is God living His own life as you. Therefore, since God is the only life you have, you can be assured that He did not create any disease to destroy it.

The Christ has "come that they might have life, and that they might have it more abundantly." [7] When? "Before Abraham was." [8] For how long? "Unto the end of the world." [9] Always remember that the Christ has been with you since God began; the Christ will be with you unto the end of the world: "I will never leave thee, nor forsake thee." [10] So there cannot be any provision for your aging or dying.

As was pointed out in the preceding chapter, you are an unfolding consciousness, and you will continue to unfold unto infinity. There is a time provided for everyone to pass from visibility, but no one should have to be pushed out of that visibility

[7] John 10:10.
[8] John 8:58.
[9] Matthew 28:20.
[10] Hebrews 13:5.

through a disease: he should make the transition in some normal and natural way.

God's life is the only life you are living, or that is living you. God is the only mind you have. God is the only Soul you have, and even your body is the temple of God. Can there, then, be any error in you? Regardless of what the appearance may be, the error is not in you. When you have realized that, you have impersonalized the error, and you have placed it out in universal mortal consciousness where it always was. There, you make it nothing by realizing that God did not create it, that it has no part in God, and that the Christ is present to nullify it.

Error exists only as an illusory appearance. Just as the sky appears to sit on a mountain, so all false appetites, all disease, all lack, and all limitation exist only as illusory appearances. The moment you impersonalize and "nothingize" them, you are well on the way to their destruction, so much so that in some cases, you will have instantaneous healings through this realization.

In other cases, it may take time because there is another element with which you are dealing, and that is the receptivity of the person. That is why it is much easier for cats and dogs to be healed than for human beings. The cats and dogs are not trying to hold on to something, whereas human beings usually are. And the very things they are trying to hold on to are the things that are most harmful to them.

ACROSS THE DESK

As human beings we find our supply in money, and our health in the body. If our assimilation and elimination function according to what is considered normal, then we believe we are healthy. We believe that life is dependent on breathing and on the functioning of the heart, and that intelligence is associated with the brain. What we are doing in The Infinite Way, however, is making a transition from this material sense of life to the spiritual.

Our healing work, therefore, is never an attempt to correct what is wrong in the body, the mind, or the pocketbook. "We cannot meet a problem on the level of the problem." [11] If we should try to do something about any inharmonious or discordant condition, we would not succeed. First, we have to move outside the realm of the problem before harmony can be revealed.

We find our harmony in Spirit, in Consciousness. Since God is Consciousness, and since God is supply, we find our health in God or in Consciousness. Even the prophets of the Old Testament knew that God is the health of our countenance. Health and supply must be found not in the body and the pocketbook, but in Consciousness, and then the body expresses health and the purse abundance. Even our longevity must be found in Consciousness.

If we try to perpetuate ourselves by patching up the body, the results will be temporary. Medically, it is possible to change sickness to health and, if that is all a person is seeking, he can find it in *materia medica* because today there are not many incurable diseases.

But if we are seeking a principle of life whereby we hope to find our immortality in the fullness of our being, then we have to leave the realm of mind and body and find our good in Consciousness. But since the realm of Consciousness is invisible, no proof or sign that this is true can be given in advance.

So, we start at some particular time in our spiritual journey: it could be today for some, and next year for others. But one day we have to make a transition from looking to our bank account for our supply, looking to our body for our health, or to human beings for our happiness, and realize that wholeness in every de-

[11] Joel S. Goldsmith. *The Infinite Way* (San Gabriel, Calif.: Willing Publishing Company), p. 62.

partment of our life is embodied in the God-consciousness which is our individual consciousness.

This may seem to leave us hanging in space, as it were, but just as Scripture says, "He . . . hangeth the earth upon nothing," [12] so in making this particular transition, we, too, have nothing to cling to because we are no longer looking to the body, the pocketbook, or the brain; and we cannot see, hear, taste, touch, or smell Consciousness. We do not even know what Consciousness is, yet we are putting our complete reliance and our complete dependence on It.

At this point, even though we know the truth, we may still find ourselves hanging in space because we do not know what is to come next. We are transferring our faith to Consciousness, but we have no way of knowing what Consciousness is. All we can do is continue to hang in space until Consciousness comes through with a demonstration which convinces us beyond all doubt that we are on holy ground.

There is no real limitation anywhere in the world except the limitation we place on ourselves. Everyone on the face of the globe can experience the allness of God because Consciousness is indivisible. So it is that any person can have an infinity of supply, and there will still be enough left over so that everyone else can also have an infinity of supply.

When we make this transition, our whole state of consciousness undergoes a change because now, instead of looking to the body for health, our vision is on Consciousness. Consciousness is not encased in the body. Consciousness is actually Omnipresence, never confined to time or space. Therefore, the moment we are called upon for help from any part of the world and close our eyes to realize Omnipresence, we can be certain that our patient will receive the benefit of the treatment. There is but one Being, and God is that Being.

The more we live with that, the less we look to the body, and the fewer fears we have of our aches and pains. We are never

[12] Job 26:7.

really separated from our health, our supply, or our happiness, completeness, and perfection.

We can enjoy human relationships, certainly, but we must never be so dependent on them that an absence of them breaks our heart. Once a person makes the transition to a point where he finds his completeness in Consciousness, the whole nature of his life changes. There are no vacuums in Consciousness: there is only the going and coming of the human scene as the fulfillment of the activity of Consciousness. When our home experience is the activity of Consciousness unfolding, we will find a complete continuity of harmony.

Until we are ready for it, this transition of finding our allness in Consciousness rather than in man, body, or purse is difficult. It must be continuously remembered:

> *I find the harmony of being in my consciousness, and it is the harmony of my body and of my human relationships.*

This should become a matter of hourly practice until that moment of transition from one state of consciousness to another when we can say, "Whereas I was blind, now I see." [13]

To be able to close our eyes, shut out all persons, and realize that our good and our companionship are in Consciousness would mean that on opening the eyes we would find ourselves in the presence of those necessary to our experience. Since God constitutes our consciousness, and God constitutes the consciousness of every individual on the face of the earth, we are one with everybody. But first the human experience must be blotted out. We cannot meet a problem on the level of the problem.

To find our good in the Consciousness which we are is to bring such a change in individual consciousness that bit by bit over a period of time we would find ourselves in a whole new consciousness, and would see our life transformed and on higher ground.

[13] John 9:25.

All that God is, I am. All that God has is mine, for I and the Father are one. All this universe is embodied in my consciousness—the skies above, the earth beneath, the waters and all that is in them—because God constitutes my individual consciousness.

My consciousness embodies the fullness of the Godhead. My consciousness is the law unto my health and my supply. My consciousness embodies every activity of intelligence, guidance, and direction.

The infinite allness of God is mine. In my oneness with God, I am all.

This realization of oneness is our assurance of completeness and perfection, and it acts to break the human ties of dependence on person, place, or thing. In one experience after another, we transfer our allegiance or faith from effect back to Cause. We break our dependency on "man, whose breath is in his nostrils." [14]

With every appearance of discord, we lift our thought immediately in meditation:

I find my oneness in Consciousness which is Cause, not in matter or effect. I look to Cause for my peace, my wholeness, my satisfaction, and my joy, and these become manifest in tangible form.

Every day, we make the decision to live in Consciousness, to find our health and our supply in Consciousness, and in Consciousness alone. After that, we drop it and let it rest, but sometime later in the day we will again remember that we are seeking our good in omnipresent Consciousness. As we persist in that, we bring the day closer when the transition in consciousness takes place. Then there are no more statements or declarations: there is just the living of it.

This cannot be explained to anyone, and moreover, we have no right to try to explain it. This is an experience to be lived, but never talked about because the human mind could never understand what we mean by a transition of consciousness.

[14] Isaiah 2:22.

SIX

Mind Imbued with Truth

———•———

Mind is an instrument of awareness. Through the mind we can know and become aware of people, things, and ideas. With the mind we reason; with the mind we think. A human being can gain control of his mind if he is willing to study and practice to attain this mastery; and he can use his mind for a reasoning, a thinking, or a contemplative purpose. But it is the human being who is *using* his mind, and therefore, that mind must be an instrument or an effect: it cannot be a cause.

There is an I behind the mind. There is an I who thinks through the mind and reasons with the mind. In other words, there is an I who uses the mind. Therefore, that I is greater than the mind.

Through the instrumentality of the mind, we can think good thoughts or bad thoughts; we can perpetrate good deeds or bad deeds. Mind can be aware of good or of evil. If the mind is the creator of thought, however, and can create good thoughts as well as evil thoughts, then God certainly is not mind. How could mind be God if mind can be the instrument both of good and of evil? God is too pure to behold iniquity; God is light; in Him is no darkness at all; and when we penetrate beyond mind, we are in the realm of neither good nor evil: we are in the realm of pure Being.

To have received illumination in any degree is to have revealed within our own being the truth that God is good—not good *and* evil: good! God is love—not love *and* hate, just love! God is life—not life *and* death, just life! God is one, and there is no duality in God, nor are there any pairs of opposites in Him. Once illumination is attained, we are living beyond the pairs of opposites in a consciousness of neither good nor evil. In that state of consciousness, we cannot be good and we cannot be evil: we can just be. The sun cannot be good or evil: it can just shine. If we are out in the sun for the proper length of time, the effect on us is good, but if we are out in it too long and get a severe sunburn, the effect is bad. Is the sun good or bad? The sun cannot be good or bad: it can just be the sun.

Mind As a Transparency

When we transcend thought and reach that consciousness which is an attitude of listening, the mind is unconditioned. In its pure unconditioned state, it is an instrument for neither good nor evil: it is an instrument for the Spirit alone, and as such it will be the instrument for revealing harmony. Where disease was, there will be health; where the fear of death was, there will be life; where the possibility of accident was, there will be harmony, safety, and security.

The greater the ability to meditate, that is, to sit in a state of receptivity with no conscious thinking taking place, the closer we come to the point where we do neither good nor evil, but are an instrument through which harmony is revealed even where discord had been.

While we are functioning on the plane of thought, thought can be used to heal or to bless, but let us never forget that because the mind is an instrument which can be used for good or for evil, there are those on the level of thought who can use their minds for evil if they so choose.

Mind in its unconditioned state is the instrument through which we attain God-awareness. Mind, freed of personal human thought, the unconditioned mind, becomes a clear transparency through which Spirit is made evident to us. In our present state of being, mind has a very important function in our life, and the purer we can keep the mind, the greater degree of harmony will we bring into our experience.

Feeding the Mind

"Thou wilt keep him in perfect peace, whose mind is stayed," not on obscenity, vulgarity, and destructiveness, but "on thee." [1] A mind imbued with truth is a law of harmony to ourselves and to anyone within range of our thought. A mind, our mind, imbued with truth is a law of annihilation to discord and inharmony.

The command is, "Choose you!" [2] If we wake up in the morning, jump out of bed, take a shower, eat our breakfast, rush out to business or the market, and then retire with no thought of God, the mind is devoid of spiritual truth. We have only to read the daily papers to see what human life is like when the mind is not imbued with spiritual truth. As human beings, we live in a dual universe: good can happen to us today, and evil tomorrow;

[1] Isaiah 26:3.
[2] Joshua 24:15.

abundance can be our experience today, and lack next year. Anything can happen. It is hit or miss, luck, chance, accident, cleverness, or what not, and we apparently have no control over it.

Those who have not yet been led to any of the metaphysical or spiritual approaches to life often have no control over their minds, and cannot decide what they will read or what they will think. That may be why the Master said, "For ye have the poor always with you," [3] the poor in Spirit, those who have no capacity or knowledge of the spiritual aspect of life and therefore live out their whole life in the jungle of human experience.

The Fruitage of a Mind Imbued with Truth

How different is the life of The Infinite Way student who has learned to awaken in the morning and at once bring to conscious awareness the presence of God, and who throughout the day follows a program of keeping his mind stayed on God, acknowledging Him in all his ways: in every way, from waking up in the morning to retiring at night, and even in the middle of the night meditating and being renewed, not by sleeping, but by communing with the Spirit.

As consciousness and mind are imbued with truth, as we make God a part of our days and our nights, gradually the erroneous experiences of human life begin to disappear. At first, students sometimes wonder what benefits they are experiencing from this communion with God, until they recall how few days they have lost from work through sickness, how few dollars have had to be spent for medical care, medication, and hospitalization, or how their income has either remained stable in times of economic stress or been on the upward spiral. They probably had been looking for some kind of a spectacular demonstration,

[3] Matthew 26:11.

some kind of miracle out of the sky, but the spiritual life is not like that.

The spiritual life is a "dying daily" to the fleshly sense of life; it is a sloughing off, a falling away of materiality and physicality, and a gradual coming into spiritual awareness with a resultant harmony on the outer plane. Any student who has been on the spiritual path for even so short a time as three years must be aware of some change in his consciousness, and probably some change for the better in his outer experience. It is there; it must be there.

The mind that is imbued with truth, the mind that maintains truth in consciousness must eventually find that a new consciousness is being formed, and when a new consciousness is formed, a new body is formed. In the human sense of life, the body is an instrument that can be used for good or for evil. It is the instrument of the person possessing it, and can be used destructively, harmfully, injuriously, or sinfully; but when we keep the mind filled with spiritual truth, there is then no possibility of evil governing the body. It is only when we open our minds to evil that there can be evil effects on the body.

The mind, also, is an instrument. We can use it any way we choose up to a certain point. With that mind, we can attune ourselves to God. On the other hand, we can open our minds to read detective stories, to watch cowboy pictures on television, or other trivia. The reason this can be done is because we have a mind over which we have control, and we can choose what is to come through that mind.

The mind is not a power in itself: mind is an instrument. We can fill our minds with truth and prove that the truth we take into the mind externalizes as harmonious conditions. In the same way, we can accept evil in our minds and make it a power in our life, not that it has power of its own, but because we permit it to have power by our acceptance of it.

The mind is an instrument that we use for whatever purpose we want to use it. There are some persons who want to compose music, and they open their minds to receive the melody. There are other persons who want to paint pictures, and they open their minds to receive art in that form. Still others wish to be inventors, and they open their minds to receive new inventions or discoveries.

There is a "you," and there is your mind. Your mind is neither good nor evil: it is an instrument, and it is up to you to choose what you are going to entertain in your mind. It is up to each one of us to make that decision. If we have discovered that God is omnipresence, we will choose to commune with God morning, noon, and night, and we will find that communion to be so joyous, so fruitful, and so beneficial that we will take no pleasure in communing with anything of an evil nature in this world. We will keep the mind attuned to truth by reading books of truth. We will keep the mind filled with the spiritual awareness of God's presence and with a realization of the nonpower of anything other than God. The days and the nights will be given to God.

Mind Is the Substance of Body

Within recent years, physicists have announced their great scientific discovery that mind is the substance of matter. That sets the official seal of science on what has been known to metaphysicians for years. What scientists will do with the knowledge that mind is actually the substance of matter, we have no way of predicting, but when the application of this discovery becomes more widespread there may be many surprising results. For many years, metaphysicians have made use of this knowledge in their healing work, but in future years it will be of importance to the world in ways unknown at the present time.

Once it is understood that mind is the substance of matter, the scriptural passage, "For he that soweth to his flesh shall of the flesh reap corruption; but he that soweth to the Spirit shall of the Spirit reap life everlasting," [4] will be understood. In other words, mind beclouded by an ignorance of spiritual truth produces a body of sin, disease, age, and death. Mind imbued with spiritual truth brings forth a body of harmony. That is because there is not mind *and* body: mind is the substance of the body, and therefore the truth that we take into the mind becomes the substance of a harmonious body. On the other hand, taking into the mind sensuality, lust, hate, jealousy, and envy produces in the body their own image and likeness because mind is the substance of the body.

This does not mean that there is a cause separate and apart from God. It means that when we accept negative emotions on the human level of life, we also accept the world belief about them as a cause of discordant conditions in the body. So, if we persist in holding to the world's concepts, we can demonstrate only the world's concepts. Therefore, we must choose this day whom we shall serve.

Mind imbued with truth becomes the substance, activity, and law of harmonious body. In the degree, then, that we maintain spiritual truth in our consciousness, pray without ceasing, hold the word of God ever alive in consciousness, and realize that within us is the son of God, in that degree are we building for ourselves a body that is in truth the temple of God.

"Know ye not that your body is the temple of the Holy Ghost?" [5] It *is,* when we keep the mind filled with God, with the realization that God is the substance, law, and activity of our being. When we keep the mind filled with the truth of God's presence and power, the mind is then so imbued with truth that the body becomes the showing forth of that state of mind.

The body at this minute is expressing our present state of mind, and if we continue to live according to the world's way of thinking, accepting the world's beliefs, in time the body will

[4] Galatians 6:8.
[5] I Corinthians 6:19.

show forth threescore years and ten, twenty, or more. And it may not be particularly pretty! If we continue to abide in the realization of the Christ as our true identity, however, this truth will appear outwardly as a healthy body and as normal bodily activity, and there will be no reason for the body to be worn out at threescore years and ten, fifteen, or twenty.

The body is the showing forth of our state of consciousness, and what that showing forth will be we alone can determine. Only those taught in spiritual truth can do this. Those who live by the standards of "this world" cannot do it because they believe that there are powers external to themselves acting upon them. They accept the world belief that climate, weather, age, sin, or some other factor is doing something to them; whereas all that is taking place is their acceptance of the universal belief in a power apart from God.

As we give up idolatry and abide in the truth that God alone is the activity of mind and being, and the substance of the body, we will quickly show forth a changed condition of body, a more harmonious one, a more useful and vital one.

This is likewise true of the mind. According to world belief, the mind slows down just as the body does. One of the tragedies of this age is the number of persons with keenly developed and active minds, who have significant contributions they could make, but who instead have been retired at sixty-five. It is true that there are many at sixty-five and seventy whose minds have ceased to function actively, but that is from lack of use or because they have accepted the belief that they are too old. They have let themselves down.

This need not come nigh our dwelling place. Every year that we live on earth, our minds will become more mature, active, and endowed with more wisdom if only we will draw on the infinite Source that is within us, and above all things realize that God constitutes our being and that He is the measure of our being.

Unconditioning the Mind

Because the mind will express whatever we put into it, by keeping it filled with God, it expresses as good in the body. Mind is the substance, or the essence, of which the body is formed, and it is for this reason that if we entertain truth in the mind, we experience harmony in the body. If we entertain evil, discord, and sin in the mind, we express these in the body. Whatever it is that we accept in mind, the body manifests. The mind itself is pure; the body itself is pure; but it is the kind of food we take into our minds that determines the nature of mind and body. "Man shall not live by bread alone, but by every word that proceedeth out of the mouth of God." [6] The more we feed the mind with the word of God, the more harmonious the body becomes.

The moment we bring ourselves to a practitioner for help, whatever is taking place in his mind becomes the law unto the body, and if he is filling his mind with God, harmony appears in the body. This applies even to our pets. The amount of hours in which we keep the mind filled with truth determines how peaceful and how harmonious they will be. Schoolteachers who are students of The Infinite Way have found that their children respond to the truth maintained in the teacher's mind, and that the scholastic achievement of their students improves, as well as their attitudes and behavior.

This is also true in our homes. It is the degree in which truth is embodied in our minds, or in the mind of some person in the household, that it governs the conduct of all those who come into the life of that family. If on the other hand we continue to see the members of our family as they humanly appear to be, that is, if we continue to malpractice, that will bring out in them what we are seeing. The situation will change, however, when we can learn to disregard the appearance and remember that

[6] Matthew 4:4.

God constitutes individual mind, being, and body. Any evil appearance belongs to that vast mental illusion of nothingness.

A little consistent practice of this nature will reveal how everything that comes within range of our consciousness is changed. The responsibility is upon our shoulders. The teaching is in the Writings, but it cannot do anything for us except as we embody it in our life. This is really a lifetime practice, and reading Infinite Way literature or talking about how beautiful it is will not do it.

Once we have touched the spiritual path and have reached a certain degree of illumination, we no longer have the capacity to think evil, do evil, or desire evil; and because of that, we experience very little of evil, and the little that we do experience, we have a way of meeting.

The mind, then, is an instrument, and filling it with truth, we bring forth harmony. Devoid of truth, we bring forth a little good and a little evil, or a great deal of good and a great deal of evil. When the mind is the unconditioned mind, it is the instrument of God, the means whereby God is made manifest to us.

Then we come to a place where we do not use the mind at all, not for good and not for evil. The mind becomes an instrument for God, and we do not use it: we place it at the disposal of God. We surrender it: we do not think good, and we do not think evil; we do not plan good, and we do not plan evil. We hold ourselves in a listening attitude like a composer waiting to hear those silent melodies. As we are thus holding ourselves attuned to spiritual truth, truth floods in, and that truth manifests itself on the human plane in the ideas necessary for our experience, ideas which are always divine, not capable of being used for evil.

Our whole work is pointed toward attaining that mind that was in Christ Jesus. That mind is not a thinking mind, nor a reasoning mind, although in our everyday human activities we do think and reason. The main function of the mind, however, is to be an avenue of awareness, an instrument whereby we become aware of the presence of God. It is then the transcendental or unconditioned mind.

We do not have a human mind *and* a spiritual mind. We only have mind. There is only one mind. That is all there is, and if we keep it in its unconditioned state, we become subject unto the Spirit. If we use it in the customary human ways, we may use it for good or for evil; but when we attain spiritual consciousness, we will use the mind entirely for purposes of good. As we go forward, we reach that place where our intent is not to do either good or evil: our intent is only that God may use the mind as an instrument for His expression.

ACROSS THE DESK

A letter came to me not long ago from one of our students, a member of a respectable, substantial family, followers of an orthodox religion, and very good people. A terrible tragedy had struck that family, and the question was asked, "How could such a thing happen to us?"

Is there any one of our students who does not know what the answer is? If you are in any doubt as to the answer to that question, then you are not studying the Writings objectively, because there is not a book, a tape, or a monthly *Letter* that does not contain the answer. If there is one thing Infinite Way students know, and know that they know, it is the reason for error. If they do not know anything else, they do know that. And if there is anyone in doubt on that subject, he is not seriously studying the Message. He may be reading it, but reading it with emotion or sentiment, not with discernment.

Even the most casual reading reveals the truth as stated by Paul, "The natural man receiveth not the things of the Spirit of God." [7] The natural man is never under the law of God, not protected by God, not maintained or sustained by God. In that

[7] I Corinthians 2:14.

passage is found the history of the human race. That one statement explains why some become dictators, while others become
the lambs led to the slaughter. As you read in history of the rise
to power of a Mussolini or a Hitler, you will soon understand
that there was no God on earth to protect people or to intercede
for them. In the same way, if you read the earlier history of the
United States and the coming to power of the robber-barons and
of their cheating and defrauding, you could not but wonder,
"Where was God in all this?"

So, if The Infinite Way has given you nothing else, it has certainly given you the reason why iniquities and injustices exist on
earth. It has also provided a way for the overcoming of these,
but at this particular time it remains with the individual to do
this. Any individual can free himself of all outside powers and
influences by a clear-cut understanding and application of the
principles of The Infinite Way. With enough understanding, that
individual can even help to free others. But it is only when this
practice is far more widespread than it is now that this consciousness can change the world. At the present time, we are
operating at the level of individual consciousness. We cannot
enter the consciousness of this world and force the people of this
world to be free: they must first be open to it. Those who are not
open to spiritual help do not often receive it, although some do
because inwardly they are crying out, even when outwardly they
are resisting and fighting.

Every problem that comes to you or to me represents some
degree of our inability to live under the law of God. This is
not meant to be taken as criticism, judgment, or condemnation.
Whatever degree of humanness is still in us is not because of our
wish, but because of our inability to be other than we are. We
ourselves, however, must recognize that every problem is an opportunity. Getting rid of a disease or of lack or limitation would
advance us not one whit spiritually unless with it we gained an
understanding of the principles involved. Sooner or later we

must cast aside everything of a physical or material nature upon which we have placed dependence. If we continue satisfied with material abundance alone, or health alone, some day it will be stripped from us. We must be reborn into spiritual awareness.

Every problem facing us can be solved, but the solution is largely up to us. Even if we ask a practitioner for help, it does not relieve us of the necessity of coming to an understanding of the truth, because unless there is a change of consciousness, and we ourselves attain a consciousness of truth, there will be a recurrence of the discord.

First of all, it is necessary to know the nature of God. This really means knowing that regardless of what our concept of God has been, or even perhaps still is, it is wrong. This is a faith in an unknown God whom we ignorantly worship. No matter how high the concept, it is still a concept. Eventually, we have to lose all concepts and reach the consciousness that God is, and then leave that subject alone, because with the mind we are never going to know what God is.

All the problems we meet in our experience are based on the law of cause and effect. As we sow, so will we reap. If we accept the world's belief that there is power in person, place, or thing, we are sowing to corruption. As long as we are giving power to form or placing reliance on anything in the outer picture, we are sowing to the flesh. We are sowing to the flesh if we fear anything in the external world of form, whether thought or thing. We overcome the law of cause and effect in proportion to our realization of this point. Does this not lead us back to the truth that the kingdom of God, the kingdom of power, is within us? And if it is within us, we need have no fear of anything or anyone.

The orthodox prayer that the law of cause and effect be set aside is futile. There is no God that can change the law of cause and effect. There is no God that can set aside the law of stupidity. The issue is within ourselves. The Master put it right in our laps, "Ye shall know the truth, and the truth shall make you free." [8] The truth is that God is in His heaven, and all is well. We do not change the law: we change ourselves.

There is an adage to the effect that when we stop chasing something, it will come to us. So it is, also, that the very thing we fear and are trying to get away from often fastens itself upon us, but if we do not put love, hate, or fear into a thing, we are free of it. This is the law of cause and effect.

All traditional concepts of God send us to God for something, and that is the barrier to our getting it. Many of our Infinite Way lessons are based on the principle of realizing God. The way to do that is to let go of God. To struggle to get God is to set up a barrier. God is running this universe, but not by our influencing God to come to us or to go to our neighbor. We can, however, influence ourselves or our neightbor to go to God. We are the only ones who can break the law of cause and effect. We begin to do that in the moment when we recognize that God has nothing to do with the good or the evil in our experience, when we release God and spend our time realizing that the overcoming of our problems is the overcoming of the law of cause and effect. The responsibility is squarely on our shoulders.

The reason the law of cause and effect continues to operate in our consciousness is because we give power to this law. Eventually, we must come back to the realization that God has given us dominion, and there is no power outside of us. This breaks the law of cause and effect, and must be the basis of our work.

Then every problem becomes an opportunity which we might as well face or it will continue to disturb us. The trouble is that we want to stay as we are, and yet have the law of God do something for us. But the only way we benefit by the law of God is by changing our nature. Are we loving, hating, or fearing something in the external? This does not mean that we stop loving one another or loving our enemy. The love I am asking you

[8] John 8:32.

to give up is the love that places dependency or hope on some person. In other words, we must get back within ourselves.

God gave us dominion. "I and my Father are one." [9] We have only to recognize Its presence, and It goes to work. We recognize spiritual power, and let it function. We do not use the power of the sun: we just let it shine. We do not search for ways to use spiritual power: we let it use us. The kingdom of God is within us. In that word, we rest. Then It performs Its function.

If our students understood *The Thunder of Silence*,[10] there would be no need for Infinite Way classes. I hope you will all study this book again and discover what is hidden in those pages. It is a radical book. It will blow sky-high concepts of God that have been built up over the centuries.

My hope for you is that you reach a point where you have nothing to stand on but Nothingness, not a thing, not a thought. God is functioning, and whatever of God is not in manifestation is our fault. We have not sufficiently cleared ourselves of a dependency on persons or things, and we have not seen that the law of cause and effect will continue to operate because we have not realized its nonpower. Nothing is power but thinking makes it so. In the degree that we realize our God-given heritage of dominion, we become free of the law of cause and effect.

Praying to God for things had its origin in paganism when the people of the world sought to find some supernatural power, and this concept has been perpetuated in the forms of prayer used today. Most religious teachings continue believing in a God to whom man can pray for things, and this usually externalizes in lack. Our prayer must be for the realization of a Presence within us, for a *realization* of our oneness with It.

The great truth is that we do not need what we seem to need. What we need is the realization of God, and that is all we need. In attaining the presence of God, sin, lack, and disease are re-

[9] John 10:30.
[10] By the author (New York: Harper and Row, 1961; London: George Allen and Unwin, 1961).

vealed as nonpresence. "Where the Spirit of the Lord is, there is liberty." [11] Where God is, there is already freedom. God realized is the attainment of the light, in the presence of which is no darkness, and in the presence of which there are liberty, abundance, and fulfillment. God's grace is our sufficiency in all things: not money, investments, or health, just His grace.

Let us begin to face our problems without a desire to get rid of them and without a fear of them, acknowledging that there is an error that we are looking at, but that there is also a solution. If we can see the problem as an opportunity, our prayer will be that we do not let this problem go until we have the truth behind it.

We work through our problems by understanding that God is. So let us be willing to let God run His universe while we turn our attention back to ourselves. Let us realize that our problems are brought about by a law of cause and effect, and then realize the nonpower of that karmic law of as we sow, so shall we reap. Karmic law is the belief in two powers, and is a universal belief, but the overcoming of that belief is an individual experience. No one can do it for us.

There is in reality only one power, and that power is incorporated in our consciousness. Because of that, if we are ill, we can go to sleep and wake up well. Consciousness never sleeps, so sleep can be a peaceful resting in the realization that Consciousness is the only power, and nothing operating outside of Consciousness can affect us.

Someone wrote me recently asking for a word of encouragement to keep him on the Path. It is impossible to do this because unless something pushes a person, he cannot stay on the Path, for it is straight and narrow. Only when that inner drive is present, can we stand fast when the temptations come. The further we go on this Path the more temptations we meet. No one escapes them. It is for that reason that the drive within us must be greater than human inertia.

[11] II Corinthians 3:17.

A problem is not as deep as it seems because a problem in and of itself has no power. The only power is the universal belief about it. The more problems we meet the less power each succeeding problem has until eventually we must come to that place where a problem is only an appearance and does not arouse any reaction in us.

Now it must be clear that problems exist only because of our ignorance of truth. Everyone who is looking to God for a solution to his problem is perpetuating the problem because God is not a power that can be used. The power is the realization of the powerlessness of the appearance.

SEVEN

Living Divine Sonship

———•———

The word "consciousness" sums up the teaching of The Infinite Way. It is what we are conscious of that operates in our experience as law. "Ye shall know the truth," [1] and then the truth functions as the law. "Come out from among them, and be ye separate" [2]—give up ignorance and superstition.

The Infinite Way teaches that there is only one power, and that we are never to use one power over another or to protect ourselves from a power. Our protection is the realization of our Self as the only power. When we make the statement that God is the only power, unless we realize that the God we are talking about is the *I* of our own being, we can be led into the false hope that there is some God out in space who can be prevailed upon to protect us. There is no such God.

[1] John 8:32.
[2] II Corinthians 6:17.

There is no God protecting anyone because there is nothing to be protected from. If we want to be free, we have to leave "this world" and enter God's kingdom. Only in proportion as we can recognize the impersonal, universal nature of error and then realize it as nonpower, only then are we protected, and only then can we do healing work.

There is no God and disease. There is only God, and everything that happens to us as sin, disease, lack, or limitation is an appearance. The recognition of that truth destroys the appearance.

God Constitutes Individual Being

"Ye shall know the truth, and the truth shall make you free." [3] In the presence of God, there is liberty. In that Presence, there is no entity called sin, disease, or false appetite. We do not heal them: they are illusory concepts, but the illusory concept is always in the mind. There is no such thing as an externalized illusion. When we know the truth, the illusory concept is gone, but nothing has really gone with it. Sin and lack do not go anywhere. We merely prove that they were not there.

It is on this point that many metaphysicians lose their way. They believe God is some sort of a power that they are going to use over error. Not so. God-power in a person is in direct proportion to that person's realization that God constitutes individual being, that it is always functioning, that it never has to be used, and certainly that it never has to be sent to Mrs. Brown or Mrs. Smith. The truth is always Is-ness, *I*-ness, divine Being as individual being, and all else is an illusion of sense. The moment we begin to do battle with the illusion, we lose the case. If we keep on arguing with the appearance, we continue to be involved in it. It is not by might or by power, but by the truth of Is-ness.

3 John 8:32.

To follow the Master's command and resist not evil, this alone would be enough to transform our life. Jesus must have discerned that evil has no power, that nothing is good or bad but thinking makes it so. It is not *our* thinking, however, and when a practitioner accuses his patient of wrong thinking, he is a *mal*-practitioner. The wrong thinking is a universal belief, and that belief we individually have the power to correct.

Every individual is constituted of God, and whatever inharmony is apparent is due to the belief in two powers. This is knowing the truth. It is necessary to realize that the place whereon we stand is holy ground because God constitutes our being—in spite of appearances. This is the truth that is the light, and in that light, there is no darkness.

When facing each new day, we should realize that we are facing the universal beliefs of the world, and they should be nullified in this realization:

God constitutes individual being. Besides God, there is no other, and any belief in a power apart from God is a mental illusion. The place whereon I stand is holy ground.

In ancient days, men believed in God and the devil. Then the philosophers, refusing to accept God and devil, impersonalized these forms and called them good and evil. The later metaphysicians continued this duality by substituting the terms "mortal" and "immortal." They still had God and the devil. But there is only God, and what appears as Satan, or devil, is the illusory sense, nothingness. When we know this, we are grounded on the Rock.

Not only is the principle of one power of major importance, but it must be understood that that power is not something external to you. That power is the Self of you, the identity of you. Otherwise, again there is duality: God *and* you. No, God is appearing *as* you; God is manifesting Himself *as* you; God is expressing Himself *as* you: you are not expressing yourself as God. In spite of any appearance to the contrary, this is a universal truth.

Do Not Separate Your Body from God

Just as there is not God *and* you, so there is not Spirit *and* matter. To believe in Spirit and matter is duality. When, through the unconditioned mind, you are able to see that Spirit is the substance of all being, then you do not have one power acting on another: you have Spirit as the one and only substance appearing as harmonious and spiritual form.

If you catch this point, you will realize why health is not in or of the body. Health is in Spirit manifested *as* body. The body is form, and there is no health in it. The health of the body is the health of Spirit. So until you look to Spirit for health, harmony, and intelligence, you are looking amiss. Intelligence is Omnipresence, as is health, because both intelligence and health are qualities and activities of Spirit. The Spirit is the creative principle of man and his body.

Many of the Oriental teachings miss the mark because the followers of these teachings look upon the body as matter and themselves as Spirit. To separate Spirit from body would be like separating ourselves from God. The body is not an illusion. The mortal concept of body is the illusion, but the body itself is the temple of the living God. It has its origin in God. Whatever the body is—and remember we cannot see the body—we take it with us wherever we go.

We must never permit ourselves to become separated from God in any way. God must function in every avenue of life. "In all thy ways acknowledge him, and he shall direct thy paths." [4] If we leave God out of any of our ways, including our body, we

[4] Proverbs 3:6.

separate ourselves in belief from God, and then this belief governs us. God is omnipresence. God constitutes our being and our body, for there is but one body.

Business under the Jurisdiction of God.

The law of God that governs the universe must govern our affairs as well as our body, or there would be something outside the jurisdiction of God's law. As long as we hold to the consciousness that the law of God is the law of our business, whatever is erroneous will be corrected.

Everyone in the world is affected in some way by business, and according to The Infinite Way, the "right way" of doing business is on the basis of the Golden Rule.

When John Wanamaker of Philadelphia began selling goods at one price to all, it was a radical departure from the prevailing practice of haggling over the price of an article. At first, this worked a great hardship on this pioneering merchant. Customers looked at the price tags, and then began to bargain, and when they were told that there was to be no bargaining, many of them walked out. But this one-price system, considered revolutionary at the time it was inaugurated in 1871, was so successful that it acted as an incentive to other merchants. Many years later, on one of the cornerstones of the Wanamaker store in Philadelphia, were inscribed these words from John Wanamaker himself, words the substance of which had been the guiding principle upon which his business was founded:

> Let those who follow me continue to build with the plumb of honor, the level of truth and the square of integrity, education, courtesy and mutuality.

The more a business is conducted according to spiritual principles, the more just and equitable it will be. As carried on today, business in a great many cases is a far cry from the ethics of the Golden Rule. Too often cutthroat competition is the rule. Prices are being manipulated in so many hundreds of ways that very few people are paying a fair price for the merchandise they buy: they are paying either too much or too little.

Although merchants individually may attempt to conduct their business in accordance with spiritual principles, they may not be able to do so in the full measure in which they have glimpsed these principles. If they consciously bring their business under the law of God, however, gradually they will bring that law increasingly into operation.

We must consciously know that the law of God is the law of our business, health, and household. What we take into our consciousness becomes the law unto our experience. Salvation is individual. To become free of universal law, we must embrace truth, and this means "dying daily." Every day we have to make truth a part of our consciousness.

This Path is not a lazy man's way because we are continually being faced with appearances, the appearances of universal beliefs, and every day we are called upon to reject them as illusion and replace them with the truth:

> *Spirit is the law unto me, and in Spirit I find completeness. I find my wholeness in Spirit, and the wholeness of Spirit constitutes the wholeness of my body and my business.*

Humanly, we are the man of earth, made up of universal beliefs. But from the moment of our first metaphysical experience, we are making a transition from the man of earth to being that man who has his being in Christ. In our sonship, we find our abundance. In our sonship, we are heir of God. But the transition has to be a conscious experience:

> *Consciously, I know that I and the Father are one, that the quantities and qualities of God constitute my individual being. Consciously, I know that my good is in the Christ of my being.*

Self-Surrender

Spiritually, we live in God. Many of us have experienced the supporting and sustaining power of God. Through a deadly disease, a period of lack, or through some problem of human relationships, we come to a place in our life where there is no material help. Our back is against the wall. There are no human resources to draw upon; there is no human way out of our dilemma, and we rest back and say, "God, You will have to take over. If You do not rescue me, I am lost." With this, there is a sense of surrender, a complete realization that there is nothing that we can do of ourselves. There is no place to turn in this particular situation. When this happens, Something takes over, and oftentimes a spiritual healing takes place. In this way, we discover that God really is available.

This self-surrender, or giving up in order that God may take over, does not have to wait until we reach a point of desperation. At any moment we can agree that we of ourselves are not making too much of a success of life, that humanly we are not doing too well, that we are not attaining our ultimate goal or finding that "peace . . . which passeth all understanding." [5]

We can come to a point of self-surrender in the realization that God *is,* and above all that God is omnipresent, that there is a Spirit in man, *the* Spirit, greater than anything that is in the world. Through contemplative meditation,[6] we can bring ourselves to that place where we realize that whatever the nature of the God that maintains the universe in its orbit, whatever the nature of this Law, Being, or Power is, It is Spirit.

[5] Philippians 4:7.
[6] For a further exposition of this subject see the author's *The Contemplative Life* (New York: The Julian Press, 1963).

Life Is in Spirit

The source of our good is this invisible Spirit which in reality we are. Spirit is not an unknown God. Spirit is real and tangible, "closer . . . than breathing, and nearer than hands and feet." We live in It, and It lives in us, governing all that is a part of our experience, not only through this lifetime but through all the lifetimes to come.

In Spirit, we find our peace, the kind of peace that only God can give, and God can give it whether or not we have health or supply; but when we receive this *My* peace, we have health and we have supply and we have happiness. But, again, if we do not consciously know this truth, it cannot make us free. Consciously, we have to make the transition. We must know the truth, and our knowing must be a concrete act.

There is a universal belief that life is dependent on the body, but the transition to spiritual consciousness reveals that life is in divine sonship, not in a piece of matter. The truth is:

My life is in and of God, hid in spiritual sonship. My life is eternal because I am the offspring of God, made of the same substance as God, Spirit. My life is not at the mercy of matter in any form. My life is Spirit and lives in Spirit under spiritual law.

If it is a problem of supply, the truth of our relationship to God also applies:

My supply is not in money, but in the Spirit which I am. All the supply I will ever need unto eternity is in Spirit, in my sonship with God.

We can take any situation in our experience and apply the same principle:

As a human being, I am a branch that is cut off, that withers and dies. But I recognize that in any and every situation I am one with the Father. My body and my supply are both dependent on my relationship to God.

I find justice in Spirit, in Consciousness, in the Life which I am. Justice is embodied and incorporated in my being. No one can give or take away justice. It is inherent in my spiritual sonship with God, and the very fact that this is universally true and that all men are spiritually sons of God assures me of justice.

When we live from the standpoint of finding our allness, completeness, and perfection in Spirit, we come eventually to a place where all responsibility falls off our shoulders, and we consciously know that God is living our life. We come to a place of resting, relaxing, and letting thoughts come to us, instead of trying to create them. "For my thoughts are not your thoughts, neither are your ways my ways." [7] Then let us surrender our thoughts and our ways, and listen for the still small voice:

I live in Spirit, and Spirit lives in me. Spiritual law alone governs and controls me. I take no thought for material or mental laws. I realize always the infinite nature of spiritual law.

God has never cast us off. It is through ignorance that we have placed ourselves outside God's government; but through an act of our own consciousness, we can return to the Father's house, we can turn and live. When we turn to the Father, when we surrender our little self, we find the Master, because the Master is Consciousness, the son of God, which is our real identity incorporated within every person.

So when we surrender our little self in the realization of our own nothingness, in that moment the Master is omnipresent to take over our life. We can never have any idea, however, how the Christ will function in our experience. Self-surrender means a total surrender so God can work His miracles in our experience. There can be no outlining in our thought. We cannot function in the human way of thinking. We must be consistent in our surrender. We must be beholders and watch how the Spirit goes before us to open the way.

[7] Isaiah 55:8.

Life is not a matter of body, but of Spirit. Life is not lived in or through the body, but in and through the Spirit. I live and move and have my being in Spirit, not in body or bank accounts.

Spiritual law governs my life, mind, body, and being. Every facet of my life is governed by Spirit. I take no thought for my life: I watch God at work.

This is a way of life. This is a transition, but we must consciously make that transition by realizing that our life, our supply, our companionships, and our relationships are in and of Spirit, not in medical, legal, or economic laws. Thereby, we are taking our life out of material sense and placing it where it belongs, in spiritual consciousness.

The issues of life are in Spirit, not in matter. Some persons live as if life were dependent on food, weather, or climate, or as if supply were determined by boom times or depression times. The child of God is not governed by these human factors because the child of God is not human but spiritual, and depends only upon spiritual law, spiritual government, and spiritual substance.

The New Birth

It is difficult to make the transition from finding health in the body to finding health in divine sonship, or from depending for supply on a salary or on investments to finding supply in spiritual sonship. It is so difficult to make the transition from finding our good in the world to finding our good in God that the Master said, "Strait is the gate, and narrow is the way, which leadeth unto life, and few there be that find it." [8]

We were born into mortal or human consciousness, and because we were thus born, it was assumed that we would respond to material laws. But now we are in the process of "dying" out

[8] Matthew 7:14.

of that consciousness and being reborn into another consciousness. In this new birth or new consciousness, we find ourselves
equal in the sight of God and equal in the sight of one another.
There is no black or white; there is no high or low; there is no
large or small; there is no young or old; there is no rich or poor.
To claim that some are better than others is foolishness. We are
all spiritual offspring, and we are all equal in our joint sonship to
all the heavenly riches. All those who know the truth are God's
anointed, or Israel. Israel means the children of God, and the
children of God can be of any race or religion when they come
to the realization that they are all one with the Father. Then we
are all brethren.

In this new birth, we have to overcome the belief that God
rewards goodness and that He punishes our mistakes. This is
difficult because for years most of us have carried burdens of
guilt, and it is hard to accept the truth that our good is dependent only on our relationship to God, and that this relationship
exists whether we have been good or bad. No crime, no matter
how serious, could break that relationship of *oneness*. There are
not two: there is only one. "I and my Father are one.[9] . . .
Son, thou art ever with me, and all that I have is thine." [10] This
does not mean if, and, or but. It means unequivocally that we
are one with God.

We have now established in our consciousness our true relationship to God. Then, as a problem arises, whether it is one of
disease, false appetite, sin, or lack, we realize that our harmony
is dependent only on our relationship to our Source. This is the
truth which, if we know it, will make us free. But we must know
it to the point of conviction. We must know that good, in an
amount up to infinity, is ours because of our oneness with the
Father. When we actually know that, regardless of what temptation comes to us, we respond with, "No, I find my good in my
relationship to God, in my divine sonship. My health is not in

9 John 10:30.
10 Luke 15:31.

my body but in my sonship. My intelligence is not in my brain but in my sonship. My companionship is not in men and women but in my divine sonship."

We are then companioning with everyone around the world who is also recognizing his sonship. We find our companionship in God by virtue of our relationship to God. No matter how much alone we may seem to be, we are inwardly companioned, and that is why we cannot feel a loss or a void because it is not there.

This will change our whole approach to life. No longer will we live our life by right thinking or by treatment. We will enjoy the harmony of our being by the right of divine sonship, and we will approach every problem from that standpoint. We do not have to do anything to the problem after we have recognized our divine sonship. We take no thought for external living. We now allow the hidden manna to come forth into expression. What does hidden manna mean but the infinity of good which can never be seen, heard, tasted, touched, or smelled, but which is stored up in us and which we know is there because of our divine sonship?

Because of the world's mesmerism, we may seem to be lacking something, and that sense of lack can come as a temptation to all of us. But we must never blame a temporary lack of demonstration on God, or on anyone. Whatever we are, we are because of our present state of consciousness, and when a lack of something becomes apparent, it is up to us not to blame someone or something out in the world, but rather go within and realize that any sense of lack is because of our inability to grasp the truth that the whole world is ours by virtue of our sonship. World mesmerism would bring these temptations to us, and so we must stop believing in two powers and recognize that "the earth is the Lord's, and the fulness thereof," [11] that all that we have is ours, not because of our own worthiness, but because of divine sonship.

[11] Psalm 24:1.

To claim our good without understanding that our good is ours only because of a divine relationship would be feeding the ego, and the ego must not be fed. When we know that God is Spirit and all that God is, we are, then the perfection of God is the perfection of our individual being. When anything tempts us, then, we can withdraw our gaze from the world in this realization:

> *Here, within me, closer than breathing, is my contact with infinity, with eternality, with immortality. I am as young as God, but I am also as old as God. All the qualities and all the quantities of God are mine by divine inheritance.*

We do not divide the heavenly good among us. We all inherit all that the Father has. God is Spirit and cannot be divided or cut up into pieces.

No longer can we look to, or blame, "man, whose breath is in his nostrils";[12] no longer can we fear what mortal man can do to us. But only when we are standing in our rightful relationship to God can we make statements like that. Only then can we say that none of the weapons that are formed against us shall prosper.

All this permits us to take our gaze from the world and live more in the Withinness, live more periods of our life in inner meditation and contemplation because, as the world's problems touch us, we need the remembrance that no man in the world can give anything to us, and no man in the world can take anything from us. We live only in our relationship to God. We do not live in or for the world. We are in God, and God is in us, for we are one—God the Father, and God the Son. The Son is never separate and apart from God.

This point of sonship, rightly understood, makes us completely free of the world because all is ours by right of sonship. Living in this consciousness is what produces harmony, but it means *living* in it. This brings about a transition from the man of

[12] Isaiah 2:22.

earth to that man who finds his good in his Christhood as heir of God. Our relationship to God was established in the beginning, and it is ours by divine right. This also reveals the necessity of not living in the past and not living in the future because living in either the past or the future is living in humanhood. Only here and now do we find our good in our Christhood.

No matter how we try to live our Christhood, temptations will come. They can come at any period of our spiritual progress. But when they come, we must be alert and be able to say, "Get thee behind me, Satan. This is an appearance, not a fact. My good is in my sonship."

This truth must be held as something secret as well as something sacred because if we voice it we spill it. The only time we are ever called upon to voice truth is when we find someone far enough along the Path. Then we can share it, but only then. We must never forget that spiritual truth should not be placed before the human mind. It must be kept secret and sacred, and voiced only when we are with someone who will receive it in the same spirit of secrecy and sacredness.

ACROSS THE DESK

In this chapter, a principle that should change the nature of your life has been presented. The responsibility for bringing about this change, however, rests with you. It is up to you to practice this principle, to work with it, and to meditate upon it until you are able to demonstrate it.

Consciously realize that health, supply, happiness, and peace are in God. Begin to work with this principle so that every time you think of health, whether for yourself or for someone else, you realize that health is in Spirit, not in the body. Then drop it. When faced with any discord, whether your own or someone else's, realize that the answer to the problem lies in Spirit.

Eventually, you will discover that you have made a complete transition to where you are living in and of Spirit, and Spirit is living in and of you because of oneness. By placing all the issues of life in Spirit, an adjustment takes place in your life that will lead to spiritual fruition.

But I must caution you here. At first glance, it would appear that when you reach that goal you can just lean back and float around with the human equivalent of wings or a harp, but this is not true. Since the goal is immortality, eternality, and infinity, the real joy is in attaining.

As long as you tabernacle on earth, there will be higher attainments ahead. There will always be a new horizon looming in the distance, a new step to take—and this is the joy of life. As a matter of fact, the ego can take very little pleasure in this spiritual way of life because it is never your personal understanding that brings about the demonstration of peace and harmony. It is God's understanding. The further you go, the less and less your humanhood becomes. The height of attainment is reached in the "nothingizing" of personal sense in order that Spirit may come alive in you.

Work with the principles found in this chapter, realizing that you yourself must make the transition. Your teacher can lift you in consciousness, but you have the same infinite intelligence that he has, and the same amount of divine love—only you must make use of it. You alone can carry yourself further and further in this transition, and that only by conscious and specific work. The function of the teacher is, "I, if I be lifted up from the earth, will draw all men unto me." [13] But the teacher cannot carry the student into heaven. That is what the Master meant when he said, "If I go not away, the Comforter will not come unto you." [14] So it will be with you if you do not let the teacher lift you up to the point where you can say, "Let the Father do the works through me and as me."

As you take no thought for your life, you receive divine protection and divine Grace. It requires a surrender of the self so

[13] John 12:32.
[14] John 16:7.

that you may receive the wisdom and the activity within. Then you find that it makes you very active in the outer world, giving you more than enough work to do.

These major principles of The Infinite Way can be found in all the Writings, but they are of value to you only as they become active and alive in you. The truth you do not know is not going to make you free. The degree in which you embody truth in your consciousness is what makes you free.

NOTES FROM HAWAII

MAY 1963

In practically every mail, I receive requests from students who want me to give help to a friend or relative, with no indication whatsoever that the friend or relative has any desire for spiritual help. This request, of course, students should not make because it is not our function or our right to give help to those who do not themselves desire it. The only exception to this rule is where children who would have no way of making a choice are concerned, or those who are mentally incompetent, or those who are sick and perhaps beyond the ability to ask for help. In such cases, the nearest relative may ask help for them.

The reason for this is that in asking for help for a person who does not specifically express a desire for it, we may be interfering with his freedom. Freedom is our most cherished possession, and no one has a right to take it from us. If my desire is for spiritual healing, therefore, I grant no one the right to force a medical remedy upon me against my wish or without my knowledge. On the other hand, if my desire were for *materia medica* healing, then I would deeply resent anyone trying to deprive me of my freedom and forcing spiritual help upon me. Because I value freedom so greatly, I will never knowingly be a party to depriving another of his freedom. It is for this reason that our practitioners are requested to give help only where a person specifically requests it or where the person nearest to the patient asks for it in the event the patient himself is unable to do so.

There are many persons who, out of the goodness of their hearts, want to see their neighbors healed, not realizing what a grave injustice they may be doing them by interfering unasked in their right to live or die according to their own standards of life.

In this present age, when so many of our liberties are being curtailed, it behooves us as Infinite Way students to be jealous of our freedom and to permit no one to rob us of our God-given liberty, but in order to deserve and preserve these, we must be equally alert to grant to everyone else his freedom and his liberty of action.

The Contemplative Life has been released by the Julian Press of New York. *Practicing the Presence* has gone to press in French in Paris—our second book in French. Five titles are now published in German, and the monthly *Letter* is available in British and German editions.

During the past few years, it has been my joy to watch the consciousness of students of The Infinite Way unfold until some of them are being called upon to teach and lecture. This rejoices my heart. I literally travel with these teachers because my heart and soul are with them, and with our students everywhere. For seventeen years, I have carried the message of The Infinite Way around the world many times, and now what a joy to see that God has raised up seed!

Our teachers, like our writings, can bless you only as you open your consciousness to them. Teachers and books have no power of their own to influence or to bless your life, but your receptivity brings forth the response. How can we be even more receptive? Pray constantly for the awareness of God's grace.

Beyond Words and Thoughts

———•———

Religion is a thing of the heart, and yet, without some specific knowledge of the principles underlying a religious teaching, a knowledge of which must be an activity of the mind, it is impossible to have a full and complete religious life. It is possible to find the religious life in a church, but living the spiritual life is not dependent on a church, and there are many religious persons in places where there are no churches.

Religion is of the heart, and no one is religious except as the heart motivates him. That is why it is impossible to give religion or a religious instinct to anyone. This is something that takes place within an individual when he is ready for the spiritual experience, or, as they say in the Orient, when he is "ripe."

One can have this religious instinct and pursue it and yet not fulfill himself unless certain principles of the religious life are revealed in one way or another, principles which make it possible to attain illumination, fulfillment, and that peace that passes understanding. In The Infinite Way writings, many principles of life are set forth. No one of us can demonstrate all of them, but if we live with them and take them into meditation, those necessary for our experience will reveal themselves to us.

It usually takes several years after we have received a spiritual idea or principle before it becomes a part of us and before we can demonstrate it. It is so with everyone. We hear a spiritual principle expounded, and we read about it. In fact, we read it over and over again, and we hear it on tape recordings or in lectures or classes, and because of this much reading and hearing, we think we know it and wonder why we cannot demonstrate it. This is normal and natural and true of all of us.

Even principles that have come through my own consciousness and my own lips have not really become mine until several years later. They did not register in a demonstrable degree when they were first revealed to me, and sometimes it was years later before I could say, " 'Whereas I was blind, now I see.' [1] Whereas before I could voice it, now it is an incorporated part of me. Now I can live it."

Let the Nature of God Be Revealed in Meditation

If you had been taught from infancy that if you were good God would reward you, and if you were not good, according to the particular standards laid down by your parents, teachers, or church, God would punish you, do you think for a moment that it would mean anything to you if you opened an Infinite Way book and read that God is too pure to behold iniquity? No, it would take years and years of study before the realization would dawn that God does not reward or punish. That is why time is an element in our spiritual on-going. How many years do we

1 John 9:25.

read metaphysical literature and still reach out to God to do something for us or for someone else, as though we had to direct Him how and where to bestow His blessings? It takes years of reading Infinite Way books before that kind of image of God can be removed from the mind and we are able to accept the higher concept of God as the all-knowing Intelligence.

Any word or thought you have in mind that describes God is just an image in your mind, an image of God that either you yourself have created or that someone else may have created for you. This is never God. There is no idea you can have of God that is God because always the idea remains as a creation of thought—not the Creator. Until you have erased from your thought every image of God that you have ever entertained—every thought, every concept—you cannot come into an awareness of the one true God. You would only be going from image to image, concept to concept, but never reaching God.

Paul, in talking to the Hebrews whose concept of God was that of a great power and a mighty warrior, spoke of the unknown God whom they were ignorantly worshiping. He knew this image was false because he had received his own awareness of God in a blinding flash within himself. God does reveal Himself to man when man has in his heart that which drives him to the search for God, when he learns to be still enough to let God reveal Himself as He did to Moses and other of the Hebrew prophets, and to Jesus, John, and Paul.

To know God aright really means that you must not go to "man, whose breath is in his nostrils" [2] for an understanding of God. Even a man you revere can tell you only of that which he has received from within himself, and this is of but relative value to you. In the end, we must all be "taught of God." In the end, the only relationship will be man's relationship with his Creator, a relationship of oneness, a relationship of at-one-ment.

Jesus called God "the Father within," but how many of us in this modern world know what Jesus meant when he spoke of

[2] Isaiah 2:22.

God as Father? None of us has any idea what the heavenly Father means because that Father is nothing like a human father. And so unless we understand the real meaning of Father in the sense in which Jesus used the word, when we speak of God as Father, we are merely mouthing words.

Jesus spoke of God as *I,* and said, "I am the way," [3] meaning that God is the way; "I am the bread," [4] meaning that God is the bread. But Jesus did not mean that he was God: he meant that *I* is God, and that is quite different.

In the Orient, more especially in India, God is thought of as the Self, and since there is only one Self, that Self is the Self of each of us. It is very difficult to understand that, because the moment we say "self," we think of our human identity, and the Self with a capital "S" has no relationship to that.

It is for this reason that it would be well if you would take into meditation the word God, and see if you can receive a revelation of what God is. It may be that there will be a revelation within yourself that will absolutely clarify the Self, the Father within, or the *I AM.* If not, you will receive some other revelation. You might not be able to express it, but you yourself would have had an experience, and you would then know.

Religion is of the heart and cannot be given to anyone except in proportion to his own devotion and dedication to the search. We will not complete our religious journey, however, until in some way or other two major revelations reach our consciousness.

In order to attain that mind which was also in Christ Jesus, it becomes necessary to drop all images and concepts of God and settle down until the kingdom of God within reveals Itself, and we come, through experience, not through reading or hearsay, to know beyond any doubt that God is our divine being, our very life, our very Soul, our very Self.

Moreover, we cannot fully attain, not even in a measure, until

[3] John 14:6.
[4] John 6:35.

in some way it is revealed to us that God is not a power to be used. God is not a power that will destroy our enemies; God is not a power that will obey our will or heal our diseases or forgive us our sins. How can we come into at-one-ment with a God about whom we have so little understanding?

We all postpone our own God-experience. This we do either because of ignorance or because we have been so conditioned that we cannot release God in the understanding that God is omniscience and knows all there is to be known, that God is omnipotence and is not fighting with any other powers, and that God is omnipresence and therefore does not have to be sent for. To accept and believe this enables the seeker to come into an atmosphere of receptivity.

Effective Prayer Is Dependent Upon an Understanding of the Nature of God

How many times it has been brought out in our work that prayer is an attitude and an altitude! Nothing could be further from the truth than that we have to have words and thoughts in order to go to God. Yet how many years has it taken before we could learn to pray without words and without thoughts? Eventually everyone must learn this. Otherwise, we do not know God aright. In this, too, time is an element.

Over and over in The Infinite Way writings the words "Omniscience," "Omnipotence," and "Omnipresence" are repeated. And probably by now, when you see those words, you hurry past them because you think you know them. But you really do not know them at all: you know only the words without their inner meaning. When their meaning dawns, then you can close your eyes because by the time you understand what those three words really mean, you have become a receptivity or transparency for God, and you then play no more a part in prayer than a

pane of glass plays in letting sunshine into the room. The pane
of glass is merely a clear transparency.

Suppose there were a threat of danger to us here and now
from any direction—an epidemic, a threatened war, or any
other catastrophe—and we were to ask someone to pray for us.
Would that someone know what we needed or how God could
save us? Of course not. No one could possibly know in what way
God would save us.

Do you not see, therefore, that the effective prayer would be
to close the eyes, open the ears, and let God in? Then God in
His mysterious way would provide the cloud by day or the pillar
of fire by night, open the Red Sea, or throw an invisible shelter
over us. Do you not see that prayer in its highest sense is impossible to a person who does not know the nature of God and the
nature of man's relationship to God? Do you not see that the
only effective prayer is to know that wherever we are, God is—
whether on a battlefield or in the midst of disease? We are one
with God, and by opening consciousness, God can come through.

Our attitude in prayer must be to accept a God of omnipotence, omniscience, and omnipresence, and then be willing to be
still and listen for the voice of God, to let the voice of God utter
Itself, and then to see the earth of error melt. If our attitude on
the subject of prayer and God is not correct, however, we shut
out the experience of God.

But prayer is also an altitude because when we can mentally
relinquish the hope and the belief that God is going to do something and be still enough to let the presence and the power of
God flow, we are already in a high consciousness. God is a
power in the sense that He maintains and sustains His spiritual
kingdom, and the moment we stop taking thought, the kingdom
of God becomes our experience on earth. The kingdom of God
comes to earth at any time that a person can relinquish and
release God in this full conviction and assurance:

God sent me forth into expression, and I am God's responsi-
bility, not my own. In that assurance, I can rest, for in that mo-

ment, in some measure, the kingdom of God comes to earth for me.

A thousand may fall at my left, and ten thousand at my right, but as long as I abide "in the secret place of the most High," [5] *no evil can come near my consciousness or dwelling place. Nothing can touch my inner being as long as I live, not by might or by power, not by taking thought for my life, by battling evil, or hoping God will destroy my enemies, but by God's grace. I rest in quietness and in confidence in the assurance that God is the creator, the maintainer, and sustainer of all that is.*

The attitude and the altitude of prayer demand complete humility. Since God's thoughts are not our thoughts, and since God's ways are not our ways, how could we possibly be warranted in giving our thoughts to God or in believing that our thoughts have any weight with God? Is there any person who has ever lived, is living now, or will ever live who knows the thoughts of God or the ways of God? God's thoughts can be revealed to us only through listening, and then they can be implemented in action, in effect.

Disease Is Not God-Ordained

The subject of spiritual healing is of vital importance today and is inextricably related to the nature of God and the nature of prayer. Evangelical healers have made somewhat of a beginning in this area and have aroused an interest in the subject so that now many of the Protestant churches are investigating the possibility of healing spiritually.

Many of the sincere and dedicated persons who are engaged in this activity, however, are discovering that they have reached an impasse. This is because they do not know the basic principle of spiritual healing and, until someone reveals it to them, they will be unable to go further. Most attempts at spiritual healing

[5] Psalm 91:1.

are still being made in the belief that it is God who heals disease. What a fallacy! If God could heal disease, there would not be a person in the world with a disease because "God is no respecter of persons." [6] In fact, because of his humility and lack of self-righteousness, it is often easier to heal someone in prison than it is to heal a very righteous person.

God does not visit disease on anyone. God does not cause anyone to be a sinner, nor does He at any time or for any reason cause death. Then what is the cause of the world's troubles? The belief in two powers. This was revealed as the cause of sin and disease as far back as Adam and Eve, and when we understand that, we have the secret of spiritual healing.

Those who accept the belief in two powers, the power of good and the power of evil, are subject to this belief. The universal mind of man has always accepted two powers, and it has tried to "use" God to destroy the evil powers. But how futile have been such attempts! When, however, through divine Grace, you can accept the truth that the omnipotence of God makes evil an impossibility, when you can look out at any condition of an erroneous nature and know that it is not of God and therefore has no power, the image of two powers in the universal mind evaporates.

Spiritual healing takes place when the practitioner or minister knows, "Thank God, this is not ordained of God. It is but the 'arm of flesh,' or nothingness. It exists only in the universal mind of man, which is made up of two powers." But there really are not two powers, and when the kingdom of God comes to your individual experience, you discover that the things or persons you feared as being so powerful have lost their power. Then you are at that state of consciousness where the lamb will lie down with the lion.

When faced with any form of sin, sickness, lack, or limitation, your first reaction must be, "This is an appearance, and I know it. But it is not of God, and I know that, too." In this inner

[6] Acts 10:34.

assurance, you can release yourself and settle back into an inner peace. Humanly, we are trained and conditioned to react to appearances and to fear them. Even after we have come to this spiritual way of life and believe we are well along on the Path, we still have tremblings when faced with certain appearances. The Master, himself, had already become a spiritual light when he had the experience of the three temptations.

From the human standpoint, it is natural to react to appearances, and no one has fully outgrown this, but we are now learning to "judge not according to the appearance."[7] When temptation comes to fear an appearance, do not try to affirm or declare yourself out of it. Instead, look straight at it, and then acknowledge to yourself that you are being tempted by an appearance of the carnal mind. God has never had an enemy, whether in the form of a person or a condition—not at any time. We may believe we have enemies; we may fear the pictures of the carnal mind; but God is omnipotence, omnipresence, and omniscience, besides which there is nothing.

For this reason it is important to remember that God is the consciousness out of which this entire universe is formed. This consciousness of God, which is too pure to behold iniquity, contains nothing destructive to Itself and, therefore, nothing destructive to man because man is the emanation of the consciousness of God.

If you live and move and have your being in the realization of God as Consciousness, you will be living in heaven. Heaven will be your earth, and the laws of heaven will function as the laws of your earth. If you accept good and evil, however, or if you believe for a moment that God has any chosen people, you have lost it all. You must see that behind this world of form there is an invisible Consciousness out of which all that exists is formed. God is the universal, divine consciousness, and there can be *no* exceptions.

The gift of spiritual healing can be lost if you believe that it is

[7] John 7:24.

dependent on what an individual does or does not do. Healing is not dependent on what man does: it is dependent on man's awareness of the nature of God and the nature of error. The moment that you see any human condition as being either punishable by God or not subject to God for any reason, you have lost the gift of healing. In order to heal, a person must be able to bring both the saint and the sinner, the enlightened and the ignorant, into the truth.

The greater the ability to relax in the assurance that God really is omnipotence, omnipresence, and omniscience, the greater will be the healing capacity because the attitude and the altitude of the consciousness that relinquishes the belief in two powers is the activity that restores harmony.

The Meaning of Faith

It is important for Infinite Way students to understand the meaning of the word "faith." This, they can do if they omit the word "in" after the word "faith." The word "faith" became perverted when it became faith *in* something or someone, even in God. There can be no faith *in* anybody or anything, *in* any concept or any idea. The only real faith there is, is the faith that trusts God to run His universe without any help from man. *I AM* needs no faith because *I AM* maintains Itself, and therefore needs no help.

Placing faith in anything external—a person or thing, an idea or concept—is but the opposite of having a fear of bombs, germs, or weather. There must be no faith *in* anything or anybody, just as there must be no fear *of* anything or anybody. Then you can rest back in the assurance of *Is*.

The moment you have faith in a thing or a thought, an idea or a concept, you have built a graven image, and then you must bow down and worship it. When you talk about faith, it must not be faith *in*. At first, this type of faith calls for a degree of courage because it means that as long as there are any negative or evil appearances, you must learn not to fear them and not to want help for them.

When you do request help, the help you are asking for should be help to have the courage to ignore the appearances, even though you recognize that there are appearances. If you are asking for help to get rid of the appearance, you are in the human dream. The ability to withdraw fear is in direct proportion to your faith, a faith without the word "in." This is a difficult idea to give out or to receive, and you cannot receive it while trying to understand it because the mind cannot grasp the intangible.

In *The Cloud of Unknowing,*[8] written in the fourteenth century, the author refers to that state of consciousness where you know nothing. Your mind is not a vacuum, but it is at rest. It is just an "unknowing" and a resting in no words and no thoughts. When you can rest in this inner communion without words and without thoughts, you have attained "the cloud of unknowing."

You are then abiding in God; you are communing with the Spirit within; you are one with the saints and sages of all time. The Master must have meant this when he said, "Abide in me,"[9]—not abide in Jesus as a person but abide in Christ-consciousness. The only way you can abide in Christ-consciousness is to abide without words or thoughts, without faith in anything or fear of anything. Rest in Being, just Being.

God is being, your being, but the minute you think thoughts or speak words, unless the words are being poured into you, rather than thought by you, you have God *and* you. God's thoughts are not your thoughts. Therefore, in order to receive God's thoughts, you must stop taking thought. God's ways are not your ways, and you will never know His ways while you are trying to follow your own ways. Abide in Christ-consciousness, your consciousness. Rest in receptivity.

[8] *The Cloud of Unknowing,* trans. by Ira Progoff (New York: The Julian Press, 1961).
[9] John 15:4.

The world has been fooled by the belief that there is a God somewhere that can be prayed to, a God you can petition to do something to you or for you, or a God who will reward you. This is a deception from which we all have been and are suffering. You will see how difficult the transition is when you sit down for a moment of peace and realize, "I have faith," and then have to cut yourself short right there. Faith? Faith in what? In whom? For what reason? And you have to refuse to answer. There can be no faith in anyone or anything, just faith that Being is being.

You can know positively when you are not praying. When you have any thought in your mind of this world, then you are not in prayer. But when you can drop all concern for this world and abide without words or thoughts in your inner consciousness, you are in prayer and you are in communion with the Source of being. This takes God right out of your mind and compels you to give up idols, the idols which men have formed for themselves and called God.

In Isaiah, there are passages that warn people not to have faith in chariots, horses, and soldiers. Twenty-five centuries later our faith is no longer in them, but in airplanes and bombs. In other words, we have just transferred faith from one thing to another, instead of abiding in pure faith—no faith *in,* no fear *of,* and no freedom *from.*

When the temptation comes to believe in two powers, you have to deny both the evil and the good in order to remain in faith.

> *There is neither good nor evil. There is only the* I *that I am, without qualities, and the only quantity is infinity. Appearances are erroneous, whether they are good or evil appearances, because the only reality is the* I *that I am.*

This eliminates a future tense, and when you are neither living in the past nor in the future, you are living in and as the *I,* as that *I* that *I AM.*

Hope, expectancy, and what the world calls faith: all these have to do with a future tense. But God has no way of operating except now, as a continuing now. Now is the only time there is, and this takes away from us the false sense of faith that God will meet our rent, or any other need, on the first of the month, and helps us to realize that God does not operate in the future. It takes away a false sense of expectancy and a false sense of faith. The omnipresent *I* is a continuing experience, not one that begins tomorrow. If faith has to do with anything beyond this moment, it is not faith at all.

You may say that you will not have fruit on your fruit trees until next month. But, if the law is not operating in your trees now, there never will be fruit. It is only the operation of nowness that brings fruit in its season. It is what is happening in the tree now that determines the fruit that will be on the tree later. So it is that what is taking place in your consciousness *now* determines the fruitage in your body, in your pocketbook, in your family, in your life—next week, next month, next year.

As you lift up that *I* in you, and abide in that *I,* rest and relax in It, you are abiding in your consciousness. The nature of *I* is consciousness, and that consciousness is the substance of every activity of your daily life. It is the substance and activity of your health, your supply, and your home. Resting back in your consciousness without words or thoughts, without fears or hopes, this is the attainment of faith—just being, restfully being.

ACROSS THE DESK

The Master speaks about praying in secret, going into the inner sanctuary so as not to be seen of men. He speaks also about doing our benevolences in secret, and cautions us not to attract attention to ourselves as though we needed the praise of men. These principles are especially important to students of The Infinite Way.

Outwardly, we must not seem to be more righteous, nor must we seem to be different from our next door neighbor, and yet in our inner life we must be so different that one might think we were persons of two different worlds. No longer can we indulge in prejudice, bias, bigotry, revenge, or ambition. These are barriers to spiritual progress, but the main barrier to progress on the spiritual path lies in the personal sense of the word "I." We cannot live this life through and in Consciousness, and at the same time keep indulging that word "I" in its human sense. The two are contradictory to each other. Whenever we say, "I am healthy; I am wealthy; I am grateful; I am loving; I am forgiving," we are indulging in personal sense which will prevent us from reaching our ultimate goal.

Everyone on the spiritual path has the same goal: to reach the place described by Paul, "I live; yet not I, but Christ liveth in me," [10] and ultimately to reach the high point of realization announced by the Master, "He that seeth me seeth him that sent me." [11] But is the Christ living our life if we live by personal sense—by jealousy, bigotry, hatred, revenge, or animosity? Is there any place for the Christ to live if these human qualities are present? What chance does the Christ have to live our life if we have a human ambition of any name or nature? What chance does the Christ have to live our life if we look out at this world with personal sense, with judgment or criticism as to religion, race, or nationality, or if we in any way try to make others subservient to us?

We are called upon to relinquish such human qualities, and this is the meaning of "dying daily," "dying" to the personal sense of self. It means that we can have no personal wishes, no personal desires, not even good ones. Our only desire must be to let Consciousness live our life as our individual experience. Then, without these personal desires, we can be a clear channel for that which is waiting to come through us.

We do not live to be seen of men because then we are putting on a false face and setting that up to be admired and acclaimed.

[10] Galatians 2:20.
[11] John 12:45.

The word *persona* itself means mask, the mask of personality. If we look at the outer form and its characteristics, we cannot see the person. Whatever our life is, it should be an internal one, and above all it should be lived in the realization that whatever the outer form, it must be the product of an inner Grace, an inner contact with the Spirit, an inner communion. Whatever we are, we are because of our relationship to God. We are heir of God to all His character and qualities, and when we know that, we are not building up our personal ego, but rather deflating it.

The ancient Hebrew teaching of sacrifice, self-abnegation, and torture—sackcloth and ashes—was based on the denial of the self, a teaching originally revealed in Egypt. They thought that by denying themselves food and other necessities they were sacrificing self. But this was really a form of self-righteousness and a building up of the self. Today, too, there are many persons who do not believe it is right to enjoy the good things of life. They think that the more pain they endure, the more spiritual they are, but what they are really doing is glorifying the ego, and the more they wallow in their suffering, the greater the ego.

If, however, we live completely in the realization that "I live; yet not I, but Christ liveth in me," then the personal sense of self will diminish and disappear. When Consciousness takes over, It eliminates any erroneous traits or desires that we may have, and It does this in Its own way and in Its own time. If we try to eliminate them ourselves, we are only being self-righteous. This does not mean that we do nothing. We must make an effort to realize what Consciousness is, but that effort does not involve wearing sackcloth and ashes.

Ultimately, we all want to be free of disease, lack and limitation, sin or sinful desires; we all want to be free of material law. This freedom, however, we cannot achieve by ourselves. It can be accomplished only by making the transition to the point where we realize that Consciousness lives our life. The only hope we have for immortality and eternality or even for living out a normal span in good health is to make the transition to where we are living not by bread alone, but by every word of God that permeates our consciousness.

I live not by bread alone, but by the grace of God. Consciousness is my spiritual bread, my spiritual meat, my spiritual wine, my spiritual water.

This is the ultimate of the spiritual life. When we can make the transition to where Consciousness is living our life, that life is no longer subject to disease, sin, lack, or limitation. Then, we are storing up treasures in heaven, rather than in this world.

Whenever there seems to be a need of any kind—and such a need will always appear as something external to us—if we can remember that man does not live by effect alone, but by every word of God, this breaks desire, and we can then awaken to the truth that we do not need anything, but that we live by the word of God which is stored up in our consciousness. When anything that involves the personal sense of "I" touches our lives, we can break that personal sense if we can be quick enough to remember, "I live; yet not I, but Christ liveth in me." [12]

More and more the world is going to look to those of us who have made some measure of progress on the Path, and so we must therefore show forth that which we are proclaiming. Because of the many and varied approaches to the spiritual path that have brought forth healing in the last century, persons throughout the world are becoming interested in this way of life. But what most of them do not yet realize is that before healing can come their nature must change. There must be a purification of consciousness. So many "selfs" must first be given up. Consciousness must change, but no one whose whole emphasis is on the external world can do this.

There has to come into this world a remnant of dedicated persons who are not quite living the human life, who are a bit above it, yet who are appearing in the world in the dress of the

[12] Galatians 2:20.

world and are participating in the life of the world. We have to be a body of people who worship no one, but who respect, honor, and show gratitude to every pioneer on every spiritual path, past or present. If we are unable to recognize the integrity that animated Mary Baker Eddy, Charles and Myrtle Fillmore, Ernest Holmes, Nona Brooks, Emilie Cady, and many others, then we have no spiritual vision at all. If we cannot honor them *all,* we are not honoring the universal nature of the Christ. We must understand the universality of the Christ, and by so doing, we will at least have overcome the error made by some religionists who claim that the founder of their teaching was the only true example of the Christ.

Potentially, everyone on the face of the globe is the son of God. If he is not showing forth his divine sonship, do not be too harsh or critical. Remember that the Way is straight and narrow, and few there be that enter. Be glad and rejoice in the experience of those of the past or of the present who have in some measure shown forth the Christ. If you cannot behold the Christ as a potentiality in every individual, you are missing the way. You are personalizing when, consciously or otherwise, you think that the Christ functions only in those of your particular religious persuasion.

Eventually, if you want to go beyond the state of consciousness that responds to every suggestion that is in the wind, you must begin to live less with that word "I" and more with the idea that Christ lives your life. The remembrance of the Christ will bring about a change in your life. *You* will not bring about the change, but the *realization of the Christ* will. It is not what you read or hear or study that is the miracle: it is your developed state of consciousness. By letting the word of God occupy more and more of your attention, there will be a transition. The old man will "die" and the "new man" will be born. You cannot heal the old man or patch him up, but by living with the truth, the personal sense of "I" dies, and then the "new man," the new consciousness, is reborn in you.

N I N E

The Nature of Consciousness

———•———

The message of The Infinite Way reveals God as individual consciousness. In the realization of God as your individual consciousness, it is possible for you to sit back as comfortably, joyously, and confidently as a baby sitting on its mother's lap. The baby does not have to ask its mother for anything, nor does it need to tell its mother of its needs: it is in heaven because its mother is love in every form: protection, food, clothing, and housing.

To glimpse God as your own consciousness lifts you into a state of peace, into an attitude and altitude of consciousness that enable you to relax and rest because you know that God is your consciousness, and there is no other. In this attitude and altitude, you will eventually hear your own consciousness saying to you, "*I* am your meat; *I* am your wine and your water. Fear not; *I* am with you. Be not afraid; it is *I*. *I* will never leave you, nor forsake you. As *I* was with Moses through forty years in the wilderness, so *I* am with you."

Remember those forty years of Moses when you are tempted to become impatient; remember the long period in the wilderness of Elijah and the three-year ministry of the Master when you feel that because of the great help you have received through the consciousness of your practitioner or teacher you should be lifted into heaven, preferably day before yesterday. The temporary help you receive may make you more comfortable and may even help to hold you to the Path, but it is the transition of your own consciousness that brings you inevitably home in the Father's bosom, and removes every obstacle that has operated as a barrier to keep you from recognizing and accepting your divine sonship.

Perhaps the greatest obstacle you will meet on your entire spiritual journey is your early religious teaching that there is a God somewhere waiting to do something for you if only you can meet His terms, a teaching that has anchored your faith in a nonexistent God. But you will not understand the true God until the day when, with no words and no thoughts, you can rest in the knowledge that because God is your own consciousness He is closer than breathing. To rest back in your own consciousness as if upon a cloud with no thought for the morrow, forgetting about the past and living in the now, makes it possible to stop looking to princes, to powers—to stop looking even to God.

Consciousness Knows Your Every Need

It is not easy to forsake the old way because, regardless of what your religious background has or has not been, you may still be thinking of God as separate and apart from your own being. It is only when you understand that God is your individual consciousness that suddenly you realize that your consciousness knows your needs and there is no reason for you to take thought any more.

Consciousness does know about your every need, even on the physical level. What is it that is digesting your food, assimilating and eliminating it? What is it? Certainly, it is nothing separate and apart from you. No matter what you may be consciously thinking or doing, under normal circumstances your body keeps functioning without your taking any conscious thought about it. What is doing it? You might say that it is God, or nature. Yes, that is true, but those are only words. Actually, it is your consciousness that is at work. As soon as you take in food, your consciousness goes to work to digest, assimilate, and eventually to eliminate it, using many organs and functions to accomplish this.

There is a part of you that is active when you go to sleep, and active before you awaken in the morning. This, too, is your consciousness. It operates to give you your sleep, your rest, and then to awaken you. Is it not true that the more effort you make to try to go to sleep, the more awake you are? This is because you cannot go to sleep when your mind is at work. It is only when you let go and let whatever it is that is governing your body take over that you can go to sleep peacefully.

Your Spiritual Destiny

Consciousness operates on every level. In your pre-existence, before you were born, your consciousness was operating to form the reproductive cells which were to be used as a channel to bring you here. Why, even your parents undoubtedly did not know, nor do most persons ever reach the spiritual maturity that enables them to understand their reason for being. While consciousness is knocking at the door of their temple, they are searching about in this world for fame, riches, or healings. The fact that they have a destiny means nothing because they do not know what it is.

But consciousness is intelligent, and you were born for a specific purpose, although it is rare indeed for any individual ever to fulfill the purpose for which he came to earth. This may be because he does not know that his consciousness, which brought him to earth and gave him his peculiar qualities, talents, and activity, contains all the elements necessary to his ultimate and complete fulfillment.

Behind your birth is an infinite Creator, and you are on earth for whatever purpose was in the divine Consciousness when you were formed. And remember that, inasmuch as you were formed in the image and likeness of God, you are not limited to your human sense of self, great or small. The egotist says, "I am great," and he is cut down. The inadequate person who feels inferior says, "I am nothing." Both are wrong. Honor the creative Principle of the universe by acknowledging that It had a purpose in creating individual you and individual me, that It had a purpose in sending forth each of us into expression.

The mass of people all have the potentialities of great beings; they all have the same gift of God, embodied within them from the time they were conceived, but they have not been taught this truth, so they do not bring it forth. Some persons during their lifetime do awaken, each one in a different way: some through religion, some through philosophy, some through art, and some through problems which compel them to turn and find the answer. It makes no difference what it is that awakens one, but fortunate is the person who is prodded into asking, "Why am I living? What am I accomplishing on earth?"

Nothing can take place in your life except through your consciousness. So it is that what you accept or reject in your consciousness determines what you are and what you will be. If you can be made to accept the belief that you are "a worm of the dust," you will not be any more than that. In other words, your consciousness will give back to you what you accept. If you open your consciousness to truth, your consciousness will give truth back to you.

"Son, thou art ever with me, and all that I have is thine." [1] If you can accept that, then this Source within you can begin to flow out as a talent or as whatever ability is necessary for the fulfillment of your life. If you limit yourself to your education or lack of it, your social or economic status, then you will show forth whatever limits you have placed upon yourself. Instead, begin to understand that the only reason you were created was so that God would have an instrument on earth through whom to pour Its qualities.

There is only one Source of true inspiration, and men and women of the arts, the professions, the business world, and of all religions, races, and nationalities must eventually understand that the power that flows in them reveals itself in whatever their particular work may be, and produces the very inspiration necessary to every activity of their daily life.

Whatever gift is given to them comes through them to uplift one or more in this world, to perform a God-function, not a personal one. The purpose of what they are doing is that the creative Principle may operate through them in order to benefit others.

God Is Individual Consciousness

The great secret is that God is consciousness, but this does not change the fact that that Consciousness is your individual consciousness. Each of half a dozen children of the same mother will speak of "my mother," and that mother is personal to every one of those six children. So, just as their mother is personal to each of them, you can think of God, or Consciousness, as personal to you. You are that very Consciousness, even though in

[1] Luke 15:31.

your present state you may think of yourself as Bill or Mary or whatever your human identity is.

It is Consciousness that is responsible for your being here, and it is that Consciousness that will accompany you when you leave this plane, going before you to prepare the way. Why not go within, then, and consult your consciousness, follow its leading, and let it feed, clothe, house, inspire, and go before you to make the way straight?

Your consciousness is all there is to you, but if you do not see that God is your consciousness, you will leave this plane still looking for a God somewhere. As long as there is a sense of a separate self, you will think of your consciousness as separate and apart from the one Consciousness.

Ultimately, at the height of mystical experience, you will recognize that your consciousness is Omnipresence, Omnipotence, and Omniscience, and then all those things the world has sought to gain from God will be found to be omnipresent as activities of your own consciousness.

When you come to the realization that there is a Source of power and inspiration, and begin to witness Its fruitage, the temptation comes to use that power. This, you must refuse to do. Rather must you let It use you to show forth the infinite wisdom, the infinite intelligence, and the infinite love of God. If you permit This that is within you to flow out into expression, It may make you great in the eyes of the world, but the moment you take credit for what is flowing through you, you will lose It. Inwardly, you should constantly realize that the Source of all power, strength, and wisdom is flowing through you.

If you know that, you will be living by one of the greatest principles ever revealed to man: the strength, power, and integrity of your own individual identity. No one can maintain for you your integrity, your intelligence, your freedom, your ability and skill except you, yourself.

God constitutes individual consciousness, and when you know that God is *your* individual consciousness, you can relax and stop taking anxious thought because tomorrow you will have the same consciousness that you have today. And for those who know that God is their consciousness, there will be no old age, decrepitude, or wearing out of the mind and the intellect because the recognition of their incorporeality will save them from the deterioration of their faculties.

Only when you examine yourself from your toenails up to the topmost hair of your head and discover that you are not in your body, will you begin to gain a realization of your incorporeality as consciousness. You are Melchizedek, never born and never dying. This, you will understand when you realize that you are using this body as your instrument just as you use your automobile to travel around in. And, just as you get a new automobile when you need one, so some day when this body has served its full purpose for you, you will discard it and take on a new one. As your body in this experience has served different purposes and functions, so will your new body have its function and develop whatever is necessary for its activity because your consciousness will fit your body to its needs, visibly or invisibly.

The Consciousness from which you derive everything is God-consciousness, and It is infinite: It is eternal life, immortality, harmony, wholeness, and completeness. Therefore, turn within and seek for Grace, for the Grace that is your sufficiency, for the fullness of Allness within. You do not have to go outside yourself for peace, health, or wealth because all these are embodied in your consciousness.

Forgiveness and Love As Activities of Consciousness

The ministry of the Christ reveals that the divine Consciousness within you is come that you might have life and that you might have it more abundantly: It is come that you might be fed and have twelve baskets full left over. It is come that you might forgive and be forgiven for past ignorance and stupidities. It is come that you might have peace on earth.

Forgive; forgive. Forgive all men, because you cannot enter the spiritual life until you have forgiven them their past offenses, and have also forgiven yourself. You have to close your eyes, look back on the years, and realize, "Yes, those years were full of insults to God and to my fellow man. They were just filled with sin, but now at last I know it, and I know it was wrong. It may be that I can never right the particular wrongs to the particular persons involved, but at least I can recognize the nature of my sins and be done with them. I have control over this minute and over every succeeding minute, and I can close my eyes now and be at peace because I am doing no injustice to anyone. I know now that I am my neighbor, and my neighbor is I; I know now that we are one, and as long as I am one with my neighbor in this way, I am loving my neighbor, and thereby I am loving God supremely."

As long as you are in obedience to the spiritual law which is love, you will never have to depend on "man, whose breath is in his nostrils,"[2] nor will you ever have to boast about who or what you are because the "Father which seeth in secret shall reward thee openly."[3] In The Infinite Way, this is translated to mean that your consciousness is the law and the activity of your being, and you need look to nothing else.

What you are within, not what you claim to be, is so apparent that you cannot hide it from anyone. If you wear a mask, sooner or later the world will see behind it. No one can fool the world for long. But what you are, that is what eventually comes forth into expression. Therefore, be still. Say nothing, claim nothing, but develop your Soul-capacity by studying and meditating, and let It speak for you. Sit at home, and let that part of the world which you can bless come to you, and let the rest of the world go by. You do not need it.

[2] Isaiah 2:22.
[3] Matthew 6:6.

You have an inner consciousness that knows you, that *is* you. If your thoughts and actions are in accord with your consciousness, you will experience what the world calls reward. If they are not in accord with your consciousness, you will experience what the world calls punishment. Every act of yours which is wrong, unjust, or evil in its effect is like taking poison or dirty water into your system. Do not be surprised if it injures you.

You can always know whether you are dealing with clear water or dirty water by what manner of love you are expressing. If you are expressing universal love, if you are holding no man in condemnation, if you are not making a distinction between black, white, and yellow, if your attitude toward God and man is one of love, if you are helping your fellow man, if impersonal love is motivating you, you are dealing in clear water.

God-consciousness cannot be antagonistic to Itself in any form, but are you sufficiently aware of this truth? Certainly, God constitutes your consciousness, but God also constitutes the consciousness of your neighbor and of your enemy, of the animal and the plant. There is only one Consciousness out of which this universe has evolved. "In the beginning God." [4] There was nothing else. There is nothing else. Therefore, everything that is has evolved out of God-consciousness and is God-consciousness at various stages or levels.

What causes difficulty is that you think you are different from me, but if it were understood that God is the consciousness of this world and that the Consciousness which is your consciousness is also my consciousness, the law of self-preservation which is universally recognized as the first law of nature would not be the motivating impulse in the world. With that understanding, you and I could live out from the Master's great teaching of love as an act, not an abstraction.

[4] Genesis 1:1.

The Fruitage of a Consciousness at Peace

You are one with God only when love is the animating principle of your existence: nonjudgment, nonviolence, no revenge, no punishing of anyone. Then you can be at peace because you are in tune with the Infinite. Nothing is flowing through you but love, and because love is life, nothing is flowing through you but life. When you are attuned to your Self, when you are no longer violating your Self, you are one with the spiritual identity of everyone on earth. To be at peace with your consciousness is to be at peace with everyone and everything in the world.

When you have attained a consciousness of peace, you consciously have to bestow that peace on all who come within range of your consciousness. In other words, while walking on the street or driving a car, there must be the conscious realization that the peace which you have found will envelop those who surround you, whether in the home, in business, or on the highways. If you are not sharing the Consciousness you have found, It remains locked up inside of you and cannot function. You can receive only in proportion to your giving. Therefore, when you consciously realize your relationship to God, look around you and remember many times a day that this is the truth about your neighbor. The fact that he does not know it makes no difference. You must spread the aroma of the atmosphere in which you live.

Do you have any idea what contribution you could make to mankind if you could reveal by your own life that you are at peace with the world, and therefore at peace with God and with every man? In that, you have the remedy for every ill there is in the world. But, just as it can function only as you can accept and live it through a recognition of oneness, so must the world first accept it before it can begin to live it.

There never will be peace on earth through any means as yet

known to the human world until there is the imparting of peace from within. Peace can come only when the world becomes convinced that it needs no victories and no conquests, and that if these are needed they will unfold in some natural and normal way.

No one can rise higher than his consciousness, and that consciousness of peace comes through an awareness of oneness with the Father. In the degree that you learn that you do not need anything from another, but that you can freely share that which has come to you as a gift of God without lessening what you yourself have, will you have realized the only real basis there is for peace. As long as you have a conviction that you need something from someone, you cannot be at peace because unconsciously a protective mechanism arises in the person who thinks you are trying to get something from him. But if you know that God is the source of your good, you can fully and readily share that which you have. The measure of peace in your home or among your associates can be gauged by the degree of peace and brotherly love already established in your consciousness.

The nature of your consciousness is divine Spirit, and your consciousness is the source, the law, the essence, and the cause of your every experience. As you stop looking to persons for things, as you drop the search for things in the external and attain the realization of God as your individual consciousness, you will find everything already within yourself, appearing externally as "the added things."

The Dignity of the Individual

This naturally leads to a consideration of the dignity and sanctity of individual man, without which there can be neither real Christianity nor true democracy. Only one thing can deprive this world of whatever amount of freedom and democracy it has attained, and that is failing to value properly the significance of the individual.

If man is willing to surrender his God-given heritage of individual dignity and divinity to a leader or to a state, he deserves what he gets. But even with all the totalitarian forces rampant today, there are enough persons in the world committed to the ideal of the dignity of man that they alone will save the world from the inroads of totalitarianism, whether communistic, socialistic, or fascistic. When man is unconquerable within, nobody and nothing can conquer him from without.

All cause is within your consciousness, and therefore all effect comes forth from you. Only through learning to live during some period of each day in your Withinness can you bring forth the great treasures of consciousness. In order to inspire, your life must be lived from the depths of your consciousness, and then you will bring forth those treasures that will glorify God and uplift man. Those things that live, those things that inspire, illumine, and lead the human race upward come forth from within. Anything of a lasting and beneficial nature must come through inspiration from the consciousness of an individual. The more you realize that the only thing of real value in this world is the individual, the more will your capacities be expanded.

Put up your sword. Stand on the dignity of your individual being. Divinity is the nature of your being, and you have to stand on that truth silently, secretly, and sacredly. Then all the forces of hell cannot prevail against it.

Rest in the truth that you are the Word made flesh, the infinite, divine Consciousness made visibly manifest. In this way, you will be drawing forth from your inner sanctuary the riches that are stored up in your consciousness by virtue of divine sonship.

ACROSS THE DESK

The Infinite Way is God expressing Itself to this age. If I should ever claim The Infinite Way as my own, not only would I lose it, but it might be that even the world would lose it in this generation. It is not mine: it is God expressing Itself in the language necessary to this age, and I have been fortunate enough to be the instrument that gave voice to the Message.

There are reasons for that which have to do with past lives, and there are reasons which have to do with this life. I was born in New York and went to a public school where there were no distinctions made between black and white, and inasmuch as I had no religious training, I was neither Jew nor Christian.

To know neither black nor white, Jew nor Gentile is vitally important to all followers of a spiritual way of life because a message such as The Infinite Way can never be received or accepted by those who continue to have biases, bigotries, and prejudices. A pure message of godliness, of the fatherhood of God and the brotherhood of man, can be received only in the consciousness of those who call no man on earth their Father because they realize that there is but one Father, the creative Principle of the universe.

The harmonious relationship that exists among all of us in The Infinite Way is due to our recognizing in some degree our oneness with God. We are not foolish enough to believe that it is a personal relationship that belongs to you or to me: it must be a universal one. The basis of all outer expressions of love, gratitude, and sharing is our relationship with God. It is our conscious oneness with God that makes us one with one another.

In The Infinite Way, there are no human ties. We belong to nothing and we belong to no one. No one is greater than anyone else. Not one of us has risen to become a god. Everyone in this work has problems at times, and therefore there is no one of us who can set himself up above others, for none of us has fully attained.

Fifteen years ago, I was the only Infinite Way student in the world, and the primary reason groups throughout the world have been drawn to this work is because my conscious oneness with God constitutes my oneness with all spiritual being and idea. Because of that truth, those who were seeking spiritual light were drawn into the atmosphere of The Infinite Way. Many of these students I could not have reached humanly, because for years I never moved out of California. Nevertheless, The Infinite Way drew unto itself students from all over this globe. This could have been accomplished only by abiding in the consciousness of my oneness with God, and by the realization that The Infinite Way is not mine.

The Infinite Way is a way of life, the contemplative way. And this is my way. I lead the contemplative life, the mystical life. I do not go to a human source for authority. I turn within. I recognize that there is a part of me which is a human being and that that "natural man receiveth not the things of the Spirit of God: for they are foolishness unto him; neither can he know them, because they are spiritually discerned." [5]

The revelation I live by is to be found in the Oriental, Hebrew, and Christian scriptures. It is a way of life that can be lived by Christian, Jew, or Buddhist; it has no special religious connotation. To me, the same Christ-spirit animated and operated in Jesus, Buddha, Paul, Elijah, Isaiah, Nanak, Muhammad, and the Sufi mystics.

God has no religion, sect, or creed. Let us forget sectarian religion and differences. Let us not be so concerned with labels as to what a person's religion is or is not. God does not belong exclusively to any denomination or church.

Let us therefore think of our relationship to God in its real essence, that of oneness, and then after our relationship of oneness has been established through meditation, the Word will become flesh.

[5] I Corinthians 2:14.

NOTES FROM HAWAII

JULY 1963

A question comes up constantly in my mail from many students who have little or no spiritual background, and from those who have been in some form of metaphysics and have been accustomed to turning to God for the satisfying of purely material needs. They ask, "Why is it that so many people who never think seriously of God or of spiritual things find a great deal of success and happiness in the world, and very often experience few problems or none at all?"

The answer, of course, is simple. On the human level of life, it is possible to attain anything at all that we desire if we desire it enough to make the necessary effort. A great many health problems of the world have their origin in wrong eating, and anybody can eliminate more than half of his physical problems if he watches what he eats and how much. Many problems of lack and limitation merely represent the unwillingness of the average person to work for what he wants. Many persons are satisfied to work seven hours a day, or even six, five, four, or less, and then spend the rest of the twenty-four hours in indulgence of one sort or another.

But those who really want success find ways to work ten hours, eleven, twelve, or eighteen; and in doing this, they indulge themselves far less and therefore have fewer mental and physical problems to meet. Practically anything in the world is obtainable to those who are willing to pay the particular price demanded to reach their goal. Except for those who inherit wealth, the rest of the world has to work, and work hard for what it wants, but if it wants it badly enough, it will get it, and this, regardless of whether or not it ever has a serious thought about spiritual things.

What this question really means is, "Why do those who do give serious thought to the spiritual things have so many problems and often fail to achieve their goal?" Here, too, the answer is simple. Those who turn to the spiritual path for material or human gain must inevitably fail. In the early days of metaphysics, it was believed that a person could go to God for automobiles, houses, or for better business, but the passing of years and the failure of that approach to life have shown the world that just as oil and water do not mix, neither can the spiritual kingdom be made into a merchandise mart, for these are as unlike as oil and water.

The Master made it very clear that My^6 kingdom, the spiritual kingdom, is not of "this world," and *My* peace—the real peace, the spiritual peace, the eternal peace—is not to be obtained through the things of "this world." Paul, too, made it clear that "the natural man," the man who is seeking a material goal, cannot receive the things of God. So it is that those who enter the spiritual path with the object of attaining material and human good must also inevitably fail.

The goal of all those who enter any one of the mystical approaches to life must be to seek the kingdom of God, to leave all for *Me,*[7] if necessary, leave mother, father, sister, and brother.

> *Leave your "nets," and follow* Me *into the spiritual kingdom where there are spiritual treasures such as you have never dreamed of. Follow* Me *into the kingdom of God and find that all these things—peace, joy, harmony, love, justice—all these will be added unto you.*

Do not expect success on the spiritual path if you are seeking material goals. Though it is as simple as that, what are you seeking?

You can now know whether or not you can respond to The Infinite Way, and any new seeker can judge for himself if The Infinite Way is possible of attainment for him.

[6] The word "My," capitalized, refers to God.
[7] The word "Me," capitalized, refers to God.

Spend a week living in Chapter Ten, "Meditation on Life by Grace," in *The Contemplative Life*.[8] If this makes your heart sing, this message of The Infinite Way is your spiritual home. Then, you are ready to begin at the beginning of this book and build a new consciousness, and all the other Infinite Way writings will open up to you as a bud opens into a flower.

> Take no thought for your life, what ye shall eat; neither for the body, what ye shall put on.
>
> For all these things do the nations of the world seek after: and your Father knoweth that ye have need of these things.
>
> But rather seek ye the kingdom of God; and all these things shall be added unto you.
>
> Fear not, little flock; for it is your Father's good pleasure to give you the kingdom.
>
> Luke 12:22, 30-32

At one time, when giving class work in Portland, Oregon, we conducted a series of noon meditation meetings for six days. Each day after our meditation the students were given one Bible passage to be held consciously in thought, pondered, and spiritually worked with for twenty-four hours until we met again. The fruitage of that week's work will certainly not be forgotten by me, and I am sure that there are others in Portland who will long remember the effect in the experience of many.

Here are the passages used for those six days:

First Day
Trust in the Lord with all thine heart; and lean not unto thine own understanding.

In all thy ways acknowledge him, and he shall direct thy paths.

Proverbs 3:5, 6

[8] By the author (New York: The Julian Press, 1963; London, England: L. N. Fowler and Co., Ltd., 1964).

Second Day

And Jesus answered him, saying, It is written, That man shall not live by bread alone, but by every word of God.

Luke 4:4

Third Day

Thou wilt keep him in perfect peace, whose mind is stayed on thee: because he trusteth in thee.

Isaiah 26:3

Fourth Day

Peace I leave with you, my peace I give unto you: not as the world giveth, give I unto you. Let not your heart be troubled, neither let it be afraid.

John 14:27

Fifth Day

In quietness and in confidence shall be your strength.

Isaiah 30:15

Sixth Day

In the mean while his disciples prayed him, saying, Master, eat.

But he said unto them, I have meat to eat that ye know not of.

John 4:31, 32

After you have read these passages, I suggest that beginning with Monday you take the first quotation for the first twenty-four hours, the second one for the second day, and so on for an entire week. Repeat this for three or four weeks, and see if your consciousness has not risen at least a hundred weeks in just a few.

T E N

An Idea Whose Time Has Come

———•———

Truth received and embodied in consciousness eventually becomes known throughout the world without any human effort or
human striving. By abiding with truth within oneself, it has a
way of establishing itself. This does not always happen as
quickly as you might like to have it happen, but you must learn
that in the realm of truth "a thousand years in thy sight are but
as yesterday when it is past," [1] and one day as a thousand years.
There will be periods of thousands of years when little progress
seems to be made. Then suddenly more progress is made in one
day than in the preceding thousand years.

[1] Psalm 90:4.

An Idea in Consciousness Must Manifest Itself

The process of consciousness coming into expression in changing and better forms is a painfully slow one, and in religion the world has been more backward than in almost any other area of human experience. Until after the middle of the nineteenth century, religion in the Western World was a total state of darkness and ignorance, almost without even the tiniest bit of light. But in the middle of the nineteenth century, some of the Oriental Scriptures were translated into English and German and later into French, although it was in England and in Germany that they took root and the first spiritual light began to dawn. Then, in the United States, there was the period of the Transcendentalists in New England and the founding of Christian Science and Unity. All these were the light casting its shadow into visibility and prophesying things to come.

"Nothing is so powerful as an idea whose time has come," [2] and the idea of freedom, liberty, justice, and equality is an idea whose time has come in this age. Colonialism, the holding in bondage of one people over another, has to go. Nothing today can stop the breaking down of racial, religious, and nationalistic prejudice. Unfortunately, the world, not knowing how to achieve this by spiritual means, has had recourse only to the human means of force. To go out and fight for what it wanted is all the world has known.

Any idea or principle, real and true, revealed in consciousness, will manifest itself in human experience. Had more persons been sufficiently aware of the operation of this principle when the idea of freedom entered human consciousness and became tangible as form in ancient Greece, I believe that worldwide freedom would have been attained long ago. Instead, today

[2] Victor Hugo.

there are large segments of the population of the world where there is not a semblance of freedom.

In its widest sense, freedom includes religious, economic, political, and racial freedom—yes, even physical and mental freedom. Man cannot create freedom: freedom is of God. It is a divine impartation that comes to the consciousness of those who are receptive to that idea. Freedom must be received in consciousness because the only way God functions is as consciousness. Freedom is not to be begged for or fought for: freedom is to be recognized. Freedom in whatever form is God's gift to God's kingdom, God's activity operating in God's kingdom, God's grace appearing as liberty, justice, and equality, all of which are qualities of divine Consciousness, omnipresent where we are.

God's Instruments

In every generation there are certain persons born unselfed, with a love in their hearts that is not entirely self-love, a love that looks across the visible horizon and wonders, "What can I do to help?" To such persons, divine impartations are revealed. Florence Nightingale was one of the unselfed persons of the world, and certainly Christopher Columbus played a part in freeing the world of its bondage to time and space.

Freedom is "a many splendored thing" and has many facets. So it is that, here and there, individuals receive impartations from the infinite Source which is divine Consciousness, and these individuals draw others unto themselves. In this way, then, the ideals of political, economic, racial, and religious freedom are spread over the earth. There will always be instruments of God on earth because in every age there are persons born who are attuned with their Source, but of themselves, men and women are nothing.

The age of material power is a thing of the past. We are now living in the age when spiritual power is beginning to be understood, and spiritual power means nonpower. It means to "resist not evil," [3] to abide in the Word, and let the Word abide in you: " 'It is I; be not afraid.' [4] *I* in the midst of you is mighty. Put up your sword."

All power is in the hands of the Infinite, the Eternal, and it operates through Grace. How do you make this come true? By knowing it. This truth cannot make you free without your knowing it. You have to ponder truth, meditate upon it in your innermost secret sanctuary, and it will establish itself externally in miraculous ways.

Every time that you entertain a spiritual truth, you are in some measure attaining freedom, or life by Grace, but because there is only one infinite, unconditioned Consciousness, you are doing more than this. Somewhere in the world there are those attuned, and every time you individually receive an impartation of truth in your consciousness, it is being received in the consciousness of those who are similarly attuned. In other words, all over the world at this minute, there are persons longing with all their hearts and souls and minds and bodies for freedom. There are persons who are turning to their Withinness, sometimes in prison and sometimes because they have no one or nothing to turn to. In this way they are making themselves receptive to truth. They have created a vacuum, and they are thereby attuned to the unconditioned Consciousness.

The greater the degree of your spiritual freedom, the more widespread is the freedom that you can give. Through your study and meditation, you may attain such a degree of spiritual freedom that you will be a blessing to members of your family and to your immediate neighbors. You may attain such a great degree of freedom that you may become a healer on a wide scale: city-wide, state-wide, nation-wide, or world-wide. It may

[3] Matthew 5:39.
[4] Matthew 14:27.

give birth in you to some idea of commercial or political freedom and so be a freeing influence for thousands of persons. Or,
you may go so high in consciousness that you bring about a new
world-wide religion. Who knows? But if you do, please do not
organize it.

The Infinite Way Ideal of Freedom

Always remember that the freedom you crave in your heart
everyone else is also craving, but do not believe that anyone can
ever be free through binding another. When you set a person
free, remember that you must set him free to have any religion
he may choose or to have none at all. Set everyone free, and you
yourself will be free to a greater extent.

The Infinite Way ideal of freedom has always been that of a
spiritual bond uniting individuals in an eternal relationship of
love, sharing, and good will. As one of its foundational points,
The Infinite Way has no memberships and no dues; there is no
binding of anyone to itself. It not only sets all free but maintains
their freedom.

Freedom Has Been Loosed in Consciousness

This spiritual idea of freedom has no limits or boundaries, and if
you look beyond the visible horizon, you will see how it is functioning in one group and in one country after another. History
records events, but seldom records the causes underlying or
leading up to those events.

For example, a cursory knowledge of the War between the
States might lead one to believe that this war was fought because
some persons so loved the Negroes that they were willing to die

to free them, or because of the commercial rivalry between the northern and the southern states. Such a conclusion would ignore the fact that the idea of freedom, liberty, equality, and justice had been infiltrating consciousness as far back as ancient Greece, on down to the period when the Magna Carta took form in England, and on through the American, French, and South American revolutions. All these events were but the outpicturing of a changed state of consciousness, which culminated in more and more freedom for the people.

This idea of freedom is now spreading into the area of religion: Bishop Pike of the Episcopal Church is setting many of his people free of their superstition and ignorance, and the late Pope John endorsed the idea of universal and complete religious liberty for all persons. Pope Paul VI, upon his election to the pontificate, announced that he favored the aims of the late Pope John, stating that the Roman Catholic church should continue along the course indicated by his predecessor. A high churchman of England, the Bishop of Woolwich, has written to the effect that prayer is not asking anything of God, that prayer is listening, and that we must give up concepts of God to attain the God-experience. These advances are the fruitage of the truth that has been imparted to human consciousness from the infinite divine Consciousness.

A truth that is given to one individual in consciousness, and which he holds sacred within him and imparts only to those who are responsive so that it makes a circle or flow between them, must eventually be established for all men on earth. The divine Presence has within Itself the power to establish Itself, if It is remembered and held to sacredly.

We must reach the place where we can dedicate ourselves to something higher than our own interests. We must rise above self to the place where we consecrate some portion of our time to the cause of establishing God's kingdom on earth, holding to the vision that has already entered human consciousenss, remembering silently and sacredly that all freedom is a quality and activity of God as much on earth as in heaven, and then let this divine Principle open up human consciousness, first in one place and then in another. When an idea's "time has come," it always finds a way to establish itself on earth.

When one individual receives a principle in consciousness, it has at that moment entered human consciousness. The principles of electricity, for example, discovered and received through one individual, became available to everyone else in the world, and impossible as it may seem, when the idea of a horseless carriage was born in the consciousness of a gas-meter reader just barely able to care for his family, he received all the support necessary to found the Ford Motor Company. So it is with any idea. If it is born ahead of its time, it dies. If it is born at the right time, it carries with it all that is necessary for its fulfillment.

Establish Truth in Consciousness by Living the Contemplative Life

So it is, also, with a spiritual truth that is received in the consciousness of an individual. Recognize that the truth which is within you is greater than all that is in the outer world, rendering null and void the weapons of this world. This principle will establish individual freedom at every level of human life through an inner communion with the Spirit. These ideas established in consciousness—pondered, meditated upon, communed with inwardly—will establish themselves outwardly. Men here and there will voice these truths and, because they are authorities in their fields, they will be believed. Then we can take the greater step of establishing the kingdom of God on earth by living the contemplative life.

The life we live as Infinite Way students is really not a religious life, as religion is usually thought of. It is a contemplative life, the life in which we ponder, meditate, and cogitate upon Reality. It is a life in which we commune with our inner or spiritual Self. It is a life which, by means of receptivity, makes us responsive to impartations from the Infinite to the individual. It is a life in which we look to the divine Source for our good, a life in which we are not enslaved by words. Too often a word gets a grip on us, and then we are the victims of that word, such words as "he," "she," and "it." The devil usually takes the form of "he," "she," or "it." In fact, all evil is bound up in these words. But what we must do is to look beyond every "he," "she," and "it" in the world and realize:

> *God is the source of my good. God is the source of my supply.*
> *God is the cement of my relationships.*

In such moments, we will be looking over the heads of those who are venal in their conduct, those who are merely selfish, and those who are neither venal nor selfish but who are ignorant, and thanking God that freedom is not at the mercy of any of these, that freedom is the gift of God, and it is God who establishes freedom on earth as it is in heaven. Then, instead of becoming angry at some "he," "she," or "it," any sense of anger is directed at ourselves for being enslaved by the "he," "she," or "it."

If we look to friends, relatives, patients, or students, we are looking amiss, and will some day be disappointed. But if we keep our vision above their heads, not looking to "man, whose breath is in his nostrils," [5] if we keep our vision on the divine Source of our being, then "no weapon that is formed against [us] shall prosper." [6] We can share with every "he," "she," and "it," but leave each one free to do his own degree of sharing or not sharing. Sometimes living this way results in persons being taken out of our lives. At other times, this does not happen, and they remain with us. That is when we have to rise higher and higher

[5] Isaiah 2:22.
[6] Isaiah 54:17.

and be indifferent to their conduct. We must rise to where we can realize:

> *None of this moves me. I am looking to the Kingdom within me, to my Source. My conscious oneness with God constitutes my oneness with all spiritual being and idea.*
>
> *God is my freedom; God is my life, the Source of all I am and can ever hope to be. This was true before I was born, and it will be true after I leave visibility.*

Only a few are born with the spiritual instinct of wanting to give, and inasmuch as giving does not come naturally to most persons, every child should be taught not only the Ten Commandments, but that it is more blessed to give than to receive. Being obedient to the Ten Commandments, however, is in no wise living the spiritual life. The righteousness of the spiritual student must exceed that of the scribes and the Pharisees. It must go beyond a literal obedience to the law; it must be an inner realization.

Live As Guests of Life

One of the most releasing experiences that can come to a person is when he can grasp the meaning of "the earth is the Lord's, and the fulness thereof." [7] An understanding of this truth would eliminate the widespread misconception there is in regard to the subject of tithing. Since those who tithe seldom know lack or limitation, it has been believed that if people could be taught this principle they would always be prosperous. This is not true. Tithing is a practice that can take place only when individuals inwardly receive the realization of what great gifts of God they have received, and in gratitude decide to share some part of these. This sharing is done with the idea of thankfulness for the realization of God's grace, and it is for this reason that those

[7] Psalm 24:1.

who spontaneously practice tithing are always generously and abundantly provided for.

How foolish it is to believe that we of ourselves possess something and that it is ours, or even that we have earned or deserved it! We are guests of Life, and Life has provided us with everything necessary to our fulfillment.

Freedom is ours as a spiritual inheritance. So freedom is a quality and an activity given to us as guests of Life, and we need take no thought for what we shall eat, what we shall drink, or wherewithal we shall be clothed. This does not place us in the position of parasites who take all, nor does it grant to a person the right to do anything he wants to do. We must realize that with this privilege goes also a great responsibility. Whatever we receive is for sharing, not for storing up "where moth and rust doth corrupt.[8] . . . Freely ye have received, freely give." [9]

We are guests of Life. This world was here before we were born, and we came into it as a guest of a world that had already been established. Food was in the larder; clothing was in manufacture. There was wood for building, and iron and steel; and there were diamonds, rubies, and pearls for adornment. Everything was put here for our use.

If we can understand that we are guests of Life, it is then not too difficult to see the debt we owe one another. We know that if we were guests in someone's home, a return would be expected of us. We would never have the feeling that we possessed anything in the home in which we were guests, but that it was all there for our enjoyment and use, and all without any monetary consideration. To the host, the hostess, and the guests of that household, we would owe gratitude, helpfulness, courtesy, cooperation, and sharing, giving and receiving joyously.

Individually, we must come to the realization that our purpose on earth is to dwell harmoniously in this spiritual household, this kingdom of God which is on earth, conducting our-

---

8 Matthew 6:19.
9 Matthew 10:8.

selves as intelligent guests conduct themselves. As we are able to do this, our entire attitude toward one another will change, but only after the Experience has taken place within. It is like an alcoholic who wants to be free of alcoholism, but cannot be free until a certain moment when something takes place in his consciousness. Then suddenly he is free because now he has no power to be anything else.

Only a Change of Consciousness Can Bring Improved Conditions

We understand that improved humanhood will not bring lasting harmony any more than a change in the political party in power will bring a radical change in our living conditions. Putting politicians out of office is not the answer. There must first be a change of consciousness, and if there is a change of consciousness in the man on the street, this will change the nature of politicians. The answer is to rise above the belief of good and bad humanhood to the realization of spiritual identity. We will then have a different type of candidate, and we will have a higher quality of leadership because of our inner realization.

The entire world does not have to be transformed. The history of the world can be changed by "ten righteous men" here and there. The illumined consciousness of one pope can change the attitude and altitude of large segments of the world. One pope here, a bishop there, a minister here, a priest there, a rabbi there, one man in the business world—all with the idea of freedom attained individually by spiritual means—can work miracles. So it is not a matter of transforming the world but of bringing to the surface one here and one there to be lights in their communities. Then those few will raise up others with them.

The primary object of this work is not trying to improve ourselves humanly. Our goal is God-realization, and when that is attained we automatically become children of God, children of that one spiritual household. It is the experience of God in us that sets us free, but when we attain our freedom, that attained state of consciousness blesses those in our household or community who are receptive and responsive, and in some measure sets them free.

What you and I are receiving as benefits from our study and practice of The Infinite Way is of far less importance than what the Message is doing in the raising up of the entire world. It must be remembered that there is no Infinite Way separate and apart from your consciousness and mine. There is no Infinite Way hanging in space. Whatever Infinite Way there is on earth is what is active in consciousness, and unless Infinite Way principles find activity and expression in individual consciousness they will not be expressed in the world. Therefore, each of us has the responsibility to live these principles.

Liberty is not gained by fighting or by crusading for it, but by keeping it sacred and secret within our own consciousness, living it and granting it to others, and thereby watching it spread to the world. Crusades do not change anything because they do not change the consciousness of the individual. Attaining spiritual, economic, or political freedom is not accomplished by the outward attempts people make to gain these ends. Consciousness must be lifted out of its humanhood, out of its belief that self-preservation is the first law of human nature, into the Master's idea of loving another as we love ourselves, and more especially must it accept the revelation that no man on earth is our Father. There is one Father and one great brotherhood.

Perceive the larger vision. Place the freedom of the world in the hands of the Infinite. Take it out of the hands of man and realize that this world is not at the mercy of sin or stupidity. If we return the authority to the divine Consciousness, then this freedom, this idea whose "time has come," will express itself.

If freedom is to be attained and maintained in the world, therefore, it will have to be brought about by replacing self-preservation as the guide to conduct with a love for our neighbor. This requires an unselfedness. The average human being lives primarily for himself and his family. There is seldom any vision higher than that. Very few can go even so far as to give away the unused clothing hanging in the closet or send out extra food to the poor. Almost all human experience is a living for the individual or his family, with only a tiny scrap left over for others. Therefore, it is meaningless for anyone to think in terms of freedom for his country or for the world until he is ready to dedicate himself to the task of bringing it into expression in his own experience.

We must reach the point where we are Self-complete in God. Because "I and my Father are one," [10] the place whereon I stand is holy ground. This is the spiritual liberty in which man is wholly dependent on God's grace. Only then has he attained freedom. He has to know that even if all his earthly good were taken from him, he still stands on holy ground, and the lost years of the locust will be restored. Look over the heads of people, and see the spiritual Grace that is Omnipresence, that is the Source of all human harmony.

Try to vision this larger canvas of life so that you do not measure your spiritual life by what it is doing to you and yours and for you and yours alone. Rather, see how the measure of spiritual freedom that you attain is the measure of spiritual freedom that you are giving back to the world, hastening the day of freedom for all.

As guests of Life, we are really only temporary visitors to earth. It is not given to us to possess anything here permanently because we can take nothing with us when we leave except the spiritual treasures we have laid up. But remember that every spiritual treasure that we will carry into the next plane of existence is a spiritual treasure that we will also leave behind. It is not finite: it is Omnipresence Itself.

[10] John 10:30.

Once we have acquired the realization of a spiritual truth, it is ours throughout all eternity, but it is also one that will remain behind in the consciousness of mankind to multiply itself. This is spiritual law.

ACROSS THE DESK

When we first come to a spiritual study, most of us are thinking in terms of the benefit that we hope to receive from it. In one way or another the object in seeking any kind of a teaching is self-benefit or some form of self-improvement. It would be very unusual for anyone to go out and look for a teaching that would benefit the world because until consciousness has been spiritualized a person's interests are concerned primarily with himself and his family.

It is surprising how many persons, hearing of this work, write and ask for help for a member of their family who has a handicap of some nature: physical, mental, or moral. But when they are told that there must be some cooperation and study on their part, nothing further is heard from them. Apparently their interest does not go even that far beyond themselves, and while it is true that this does not happen in every case, most persons are to a greater or lesser degree seeking only to benefit themselves.

But this should not ever be true of Infinite Way students because almost from the very beginning, as part of The Infinite Way message, students have been instructed to carry on world work. As a result, groups have been formed all over the world, working secretly and sacredly to bring to light the spiritual age. The very fact that today we have an Infinite Way must indicate that the time has come on earth for such a transition in consciousness, a change that takes place when our consciousness is open purely to receive the awareness of the indwelling Christ, without any reason for doing so. As long as we are living by the Ten Commandments and the Sermon on the Mount alone, we are still living by the letter of truth. But we can move from the letter of truth at any moment that our meditations contain no thought of self-improvement or self-betterment.

In the early 1900s, the electrical wizard Steinmetz said that the secret of spiritual power would be revealed in this century. His prediction is about to be realized because the age now drawing to a close has not only given the world great scientific discoveries and inventions, but it has also given it the letter of truth. The letter of truth includes those principles with which most of us are familiar, and which are hidden in the Ten Commandments and the Sermon on the Mount.

Human beings are so completely centered in, and circumscribed by, themselves, however, that honesty and integrity are not natural to them. Self-preservation, rather than honesty and integrity, is usually accepted as the first law of human nature. It was even thought necessary to command us to love our fathers and mothers—even that is not natural to human beings, and so it has had to be drilled into them.

There is an entirely different attitude, however, among those persons who follow the Christ-way of life. To them it is normal and natural to love their neighbors as themselves, for they have evolved out of the self-preservation state of consciousness. They have come to a place in their development that can be described as Christ-consciousness. This is the consciousness that normally and naturally prays for the enemy and forgives seventy times seven. This consciousness has no trace of revenge or punishment, of an eye for an eye and a tooth for a tooth.

If at any time we turn to God to fulfill a desire, even a good one, we have not yet spiritualized our consciousness because spiritual consciousness is a consciousness that gives no power to anything or anybody. It does not need a God-power. This is not doing away with God: it is a recognition that God is; it is a complete relaxing in God.

The consciousness that does not fear external powers is the God-presence and the God-power, and this is spiritual power. A complete relaxing from power, from desiring power, or from trying to contact power leaves us in a state of *is,* and this is spiritual power *released.*

As long as there are persons fighting evil conditions, there will be evil conditions to fight because the mind that believes in two powers is still creating conditions of good and evil. Only when we withdraw power from them, when we cease fighting them, will these evil powers cease to be.

The world work in which Infinite Way students engage is not fighting evil persons or evil conditions: it is withdrawing power from them, and the students becoming such clear transparencies that the Christ can flow through their consciousness and dissolve the pictures of sense. Infinite Way students do not pray for peace or temporary good. Their prayer for the world is the realization of the nonpower of the carnal mind and the nature of God as individual consciousness.

Universal human consciousness is what constitutes the belief in two powers, and thereby creates the conditions of this world; but it is the individual's recognition of the nonpower of this universal carnal mind with its pictures that releases the Christ into human experience. Every time that we have an experience that proves the nonpower of anything to which the world gives power, we are not only lessening the universal belief, but we are making it possible for somebody, somewhere, to pick up what we have loosed into consciousness.

The fifty or sixty thousand of us who are studying The Infinite Way and who in some degree are impersonalizing good and evil are responsible for others picking up that very principle because there is only one Consciousness. This is a principle of life not yet known to the world at large, but understood by students of The Infinite Way through their study of its teaching. The effects of this principle have been felt throughout all known time, but the principle itself had not been revealed.

The Infinite Way is one of the first of the purely mystical teachings of modern days. It is enlightened consciousness appearing in human experience as the consciousness of those individuals ready for it. But an activity of God, Truth revealing Itself in human consciousness, could not be limited to the few who write or read its message. Actually, we are but transparencies through which this message must reach the entire world.

You can witness that this is what is happening. Everywhere individuals are receiving these impartations, and books are being written setting forth ideas new to those who are not Infinite Way students. These are now reaching human consciousness on a world-wide basis.

What you are reading about in the newspapers is just the product of the good and bad karmic influences of past generations. What is happening in the world everywhere is of a freeing nature, and while the world is not aware of the significance of events taking place now, twenty or thirty years from now it will be seeing their significance as people read accounts of these events in their history books.

There is ample proof that the principle of impersonalization is being loosed in consciousness and, as we continue our work, it is inevitable that this principle will show up in one place and then in another. The late Pope John made innovations which, if understood, would startle the world, and they are an indication of the degree to which he was responsive to whatever spiritual truth is active in consciousness. That this is true is evident from a quotation from a newspaper article by Walter Lippmann:

In reaching out beyond the clergy and the faithful of his own church to all men of good will, including the declared enemies of his church, the Pope has based the argument of his message not on revelation and the inspired teachings of the church, but *upon a philosophical principle.*

"One must never," says the Pope, "confuse error and a person who errs. . . . The person who errs is always and above all a human being, and he retains in every case his dignity as a human person, and he must be always regarded and treated in accordance with that lofty dignity.

"Besides, in every human being there is a need that is congenital to his nature and never becomes extinguished, compelling him to break through the web of error and open his mind to the knowledge of truth."

The Pope's encyclical seems to have been timed after deciding that the "moment has arrived . . . when it is honorable and useful" to restate the old philosophy for the modern age.[11]

Here is the principle of the divinity of man even when he is a sinner, and here is the principle of impersonalization, which, to my knowledge, has not been incorporated in any religious teaching since the Master's day. The Master used the principle of impersonalization in all his teaching when he said, "Who made me a judge . . . over you? [12] . . . Neither do I condemn thee.[13] . . . Father, forgive them; for they know not what they do." [14]

Can it be merely coincidence that the Pope's Easter message was given approximately in the same month in which Bishop Robinson's paperback edition of *Honest to God* was released? Is it merely coincidental that spiritual healing is becoming such an important subject in the churches today? Or, is all this the result of the world work which has been carried on over a period of years?

The children of future generations will probably wonder how anyone could have indulged in such a relic of the Dark Ages as personalization, and, surprisingly enough, they will undoubtedly benefit more from this teaching than those of the present generation. This is because coming generations will be born into a higher spiritual level of consciousness than that into which we were born. Those who are born into that higher consciousness will not be brought up, as we have been, with the idea of self-benefit.

Once we perceive that the only power there is, is the power of our own consciousness, how then would it be possible to fear

[11] Reprinted by permission of the Los Angeles Times Syndicate.
[12] Luke 12:14.
[13] John 8:11.
[14] Luke 23:34.

what mortal man can do to us? How can we speak of omnipotent Omnipresence and, at the same time, be subject to universal beliefs?

The only reason we suffer from anything is because of a universal malpractice, arising out of the carnal mind which is comprised of all the theories and beliefs of a mental or material nature. All evil is the projection of the carnal mind, the belief in two powers. The antidote is the recognition of nonpower, and the degree of awareness of this nonpower is the measure of our progress into spiritual consciousness.

These truths are stated clearly in the Writings, but when it comes to living them, we have not even begun to scratch the surface. The development of spiritual consciousness begins when we release all concepts of God in the recognition that the *I* that is seeking God is God. Then, when we sit down in meditation, we take no thought for any condition of the world or any person of the world, and become a state of receptivity so as to hear the still small voice: "Who convinceth me of sin? Who convinceth me of any presence or power but the One which I am?"

Watch that you do not have that One separate and apart from *I AM,* or you are then out of focus. Watch that you do not have concepts of God, because this is a projection of an image, and that is idolatry.

The more these Infinite Way principles are recognized by persons outside The Infinite Way, the more you will know that this work is permeating human consciousness. Probably all the people in the churches who are engaged in world-wide prayer activity are praying for peace on earth. But peace can never come to earth as long as man's consciousness remains what it is today. What good would peace be as long as consciousness remains at the human level? It would mean only an interval between wars. First, man's consciousness must change.

So, when we are doing our world work, let us hold to our two major principles that God constitutes individual consciousness, and that the carnal mind is not power but is the "arm of flesh" or nothingness. Then we shall witness a change in individual consciousness, and future generations will be born into that higher state of consciousness.

Spiritual consciousness, then, is one that is not warring with evil, nor is it believing that spiritual power can be used. It is recognizing spiritual power as divine Grace. Think a great deal on the term "spiritual power," and try to get a clearer comprehension of what it really means. Remember that it is not a power over anything or anybody; it is not a power to be used. Spiritual power is not a temporal power. Spiritual power is a state of Grace.

ELEVEN

Transcending Karmic Law

---•---

In The Infinite Way writings, you will notice that attention is focused, not primarily on healing you or improving your life, but on revealing principles whereby you can live better and live more happily, and this means any "you" who finds these principles, any "you" anywhere in the world. All my life my concern has been with principles, the principles whereby men can live more joyously, not only those who find my way of life, but all men: men of all races and religions, the rich and the poor, the literate and the illiterate.

After I had been in the healing practice for about five years, I had an experience which intensified my search for these principles. I became very ill, and the practicioner who was taking care of me felt that I was not responding to the treatment and would probably pass on during the night. Within me, too, the feeling was particularly strong that it would be within the next few hours. But then, in the middle of the night my mother and a favorite aunt, both of whom had passed on some years before, came to my bedside and told me that I was not to fear the transition, that it would be joyous, but because it would be a new experience for me, they were standing close to me to help make easy my way across.

Suddenly I said, "No, Mother, I am not going. So far I have done nothing in this world to justify the birth pangs that you endured to bring me here, and I cannot go on without fulfilling myself. True, I have been the instrument for the healing of a few hundred persons of their ills but, even though it were ten thousand or three million, that is no accomplishment. No, I must stay here and find a reason and a purpose for living."

The following morning I awakened so much better that I was able to go to my office. Then I discovered why I did not feel overjoyed because a few hundred persons had been healed, and why even if ten thousand persons were healed it would bring me no satisfaction. I have never been interested in that phase of life—benefiting a few hundred or a few thousand persons. The only thing that can be of real benefit to the people of this world is to seize hold of principles by which to live.

So it was that in late 1938 the Voice told me that I must find the secret of the impersonal Christ and impersonal healing, and in 1941, I started out on a trip with this purpose in mind, a trip which was supposed to last two months, but which lasted five.

Enlightenment, not only spiritual but intellectual enlightenment, is comparatively recent. When you consider that there was not even an alphabet until a few thousand years ago, and that Gutenberg did not invent his movable type until the fifteenth century, you can understand how few literate people there were in those days. The great advances in science, too, are all comparatively recent. Even the telephone and the radio have come forth in this generation, and during my lifetime I have known what it is to live in a home lighted with oil lamps. Flying is so recent that I can remember when the Wright brothers flew their first airplane at Kitty Hawk. But even though the world has made considerable progress in the direction of human enlightenment, it is only on the threshold of spiritual revelation, and in spiritual realization we have not yet reached the twenty-four seconds of the Wright brothers' first flight.

Karmic Law Operates in Human Consciousness

An area in which greater enlightenment is needed is in that of karmic law. In the Oriental Scriptures, which predate Christian Scriptures, karmic law, or the law of cause and effect, is a major teaching. This law has held some parts of the Orient in such intellectual and spiritual barrenness that to this very day millions upon millions of people are making no effort to improve their lot because of the belief that it is a part of their karma to suffer in this lifetime, and possibly in many lifetimes to come, until their karma has "worked iself out" in their life.

This same idea is taught in Christian Scripture in the as-ye-sow-so-shall-ye-reap doctrine. There are millions of persons who suffer from guilt complexes because of some sin of omission or commission, persons who are unable to release themselves. Many resign themselves to sin, disease, false appetites, or death because of their acceptance of the karmic law of cause and effect.

It is true that as a human being you cannot escape karmic law. The good that flows out from you is the bread that you cast upon the waters, and that is what comes back to you—with bread and butter and all the other goodies on it. The ignorance of truth that you sow is also what you reap. That is the bread that comes back sour. This is not because God is rewarding or punishing you, for whether you believe it or not, there is no God sitting around concerning Itself with you as a human being.

A correct understanding of the true meaning of karmic law

reveals that God has nothing to do with the good that happens to you, nor has He anything to do with the evil. God does not punish you, and God does not reward you. Whatever is being done to you, you are doing to yourself. This law under which you are living is not the law of God. It is the law given by Moses: "Honour thy father and thy mother. . . . Thou shalt not kill. . . . Thou shalt not commit adultery. . . . Thou shalt not steal.[1] . . . Vengeance is mine; I will repay, saith the Lord."[2] Such laws are desirable in the human picture because if there were no laws governing conduct human beings would operate from the standpoint of license rather than liberty.

As long as you are living under the law it is foolish to believe that you can escape the penalty for its violation. While you are in the midst of material thinking and material indulgences, do not be surprised if you reap material evil as well as material good.

In other words, there is a karmic law in the human world, a law of cause and effect, and if you violate it you suffer from that violation. Unfortunately, there may be times when you do not know that you are violating this law. In fact, you may be violating it continuously—ignorantly, it is true, but nevertheless violating it, and that leaves you with a sense of hopelessness.

But there is hope. Regardless of what your sins of omission or commission have been, what your errors of materiality were and are, or under what material laws you have brought yourself, they can be ended in any second by one touch of Grace. But then you must go and sin no more. If you go back to the same state of consciousness that brought you into these errors, you will bring upon yourself the same results—only seven times worse because now you know better.

[1] Exodus 20:12-15.
[2] Romans 12:19.

New Light on Karmic Law

"For he that soweth to his flesh shall of the flesh reap corruption" [3] means that as you follow a materialistic state of consciousness, you will reap materiality—not necessarily bad materiality because it can be good materiality, but whether good or bad, it will be materiality. It will not be spirituality. But when you sow to the Spirit, that is quite a different thing. It does not say that you will reap good then: it says, "He that soweth to the Spirit shall of the Spirit reap life everlasting" [4]—eternality or immortality.

In the degree that you know the truth, the truth will make you free of material sense; but in the degree that you indulge in material sense, even good material sense, you will be reaping material sense: sometimes good, sometimes evil. This is karmic law. But remember, you are under karmic law only until that time when you achieve the realization of Grace.

Although The Infinite Way sheds a whole new light on the teaching of karma and karmic law, few students have perceived the difference between the traditional approach to this subject and that of The Infinite Way, which teaches that when you rise above human consciousness into spiritual consciousness, there is no karmic law; there is no law of cause and effect; there is no law of as-ye-sow-so-shall-ye-reap. These are superstitions and illusions of the human mind; these are beliefs created by man.

For generations there has been a belief, almost a law, that sitting in a draft or getting your feet wet would cause you to catch cold. But in the August 1963 issue of *Reader's Digest* there is an article written by Dr. Louis Lasagna, Associate Professor, Johns Hopkins Medical School, stating that sitting in a

[3] Galatians 6:8.
[4] Galatians 6:8.

draft or getting your feet wet is no longer recognized by the medical profession as a cause of colds.

The question then arises, "Has no one ever caught cold by sitting in a draft or by getting his feet wet?" Of course, millions have, not because of the draft and not because of wet feet, but by having been brought under the belief in that law. Yet today this is no longer recognized as a law.

And so, if *materia medica* can change its mind about that law and other laws, those in the metaphysical world will have to admit that they too have been wrong about some of their pet theories. One area of misinterpretation has been in the as-ye-sow-so-shall-ye-reap maxim. As-ye-sow-so-shall-ye-reap, or karmic law, operates only on the human level of consciousness. To the fourth dimensional consciousness, there is no karmic law.

Every one of you has witnessed karmic law being broken over and over again. Every time an infectious or a hereditary disease has been overcome by metaphysical treatment, the law of cause and effect has been broken, and it has been proved that there is no such law. In spiritual consciousness there is no law of disease, no law of cause and effect, no law of as-ye-sow-so-shall-ye-reap.

But even though in a measure we are all under karmic law it is not the ultimate of your life or mine because in the degree that Grace has touched us we are free from it. We suffer less from infection and contagion, less from depressions and boom times, and less from changes in the political or economic systems. To some extent, those of you who have come as far in spiritual unfoldment as to be reading this book are under Grace; but even if you have not attained the fullness of a life by Grace, each one of you should by this time know how to overcome the effects of karmic law.

If someone comes to you ill because of the operation of a material law of one sort or another—through sin, false appetite, or false desire—most of you know that as you retire into your inner being and touch the Spirit you set him free, and the person is healed of the cold, tuberculosis, or cancer, of the alcoholism, gambling, or drug addiction, or even of physical deformities.

Suffering is the result of a violation of karmic law, and if, through your illumined state of consciousness, you are able to set a person free, you have broken karmic law. Through Grace, through being touched by the Spirit of God, you have removed this person from the penalty of the law. Every time that you are an instrument through which a healing takes place, every time that a person touches your consciousness and achieves any measure of freedom, every time that someone is healed of a disease from which he suffers through the violation of law, your realization of divine Grace has freed him from the effects of karmic law. Every time you bring the power of Grace to bear in the experience of someone who has sinned and, to human sense, is paying the penalty, he is set free from the effects of his own sins through the power of Grace.

The great wisdom revealed by The Infinite Way in the healing of the sick and the reforming of the sinner is that in dealing with a patient you have to rise far above taking cognizance as to whether he is reaping to the flesh or reaping to the Spirit. As a matter of fact, you have to leave your patient alone. You cannot take him into your thought. It should make no difference to you whether you are treating a saint or a sinner, or whether you are treating a person with a slight cold or one in the last stages of cancer. You have to forget all that, and inside your own being rise above cause and effect until you reach that kingdom of God within. Then the Christ takes over, and that Spirit of God, the same spirit "that raised up Jesus from the dead," [5] will quicken your mortal body and that of your patient or your student.

Some of us have witnessed this power of Grace in our work in prisons. We have seen prisoners being punished for things for which humanly they should be punished, but who, when some

[5] Romans 8:11.

impulse in them turned them to a seeking for God, were paroled, pardoned, or in one way or another set free from the sentence imposed upon them. Karmic law would have held them in bondage to their crimes and, according to standards of human justice, they would have served out the full term of their sentence in prison. Not so under the divine law of forgiving seventy times seven, of no condemnation.

It is divine Grace that sets a man free from the penalties that are his due, from the legal or physical penalties that he has incurred through his actions. It is through Grace that these laws are set aside. From your own experience and from the experience of those around you, you know that spiritual realization has set people free when they have come under penalty for violating medical laws and have thereby perhaps contracted pneumonia or a fever. Grace has transcended the law.

Many years ago the unfoldment came to me that karmic law operates in the experience of every human being. In that human state of consciousness which lives under the law of cause and effect, every move that is made, conscious, unconscious, or subconscious, takes its toll. Moreover, if a person holds another in bondage to karmic law, he himself is also under it, and he will pay the penalty.

How to Come Out from the Law into Grace

As those in need of help come to you, it is easy to see that the law of cause and effect is operating. Whatever the ill or discord, it is the result of a universal karmic law. Then comes your part in freeing them and being freed yourself. Even though as a human being you are under the law, once you have recognized the fact that you suffer only because of the universal acceptance of karmic law, you drop the law. How do you do that? By recognizing that the law of cause and effect is not power: Grace alone is power. The law operates only in belief, and a violation of law is only a belief.

The very moment you realize that you live by Grace, the temptation to do anything of an untoward nature—to lie, steal, or commit other crimes—goes out the window. When you understand that you do not live by bread alone, why steal bread? When you come to the realization that you do not live by money alone, why be avaricious? In the moment that you realize that you do not gain satisfaction from the external world in the form of supply, pleasure, or companionship, you are under Grace, and you are free.

You can bring yourself under Grace in this minute if you are able or willing to relinquish the desire for anything or anybody in the world in the realization, "I live by Grace, by the grace of God, not the grace of man." In the second that you have recognized that you have no external needs, you have risen above the law and have come under Grace. That does not mean that you will not enjoy companionship when it comes; it does not mean you will not enjoy a home; it does not mean you will not have money to spend: it means that you do not *need* any of these things because you are living by Grace.

You may have thought that Grace was something you sat around waiting for God to bestow upon you. No, you do not have to wait for Grace. You can move out from under the law this minute. All that is necessary is to relinquish your desires, and you are under Grace. You do not have to reach out physically or mentally—just relinquish your belief that you need anything in the realization that God knows your need before you do, and you have thereby placed yourself under Grace. The very moment you know that you are one with God—joint-heir with Christ in God, living in your oneness with God, realizing that you do not need anything or anybody—you are under Grace. Only do not go back and sin again; do not go back tomorrow to a fear of lack, of sin, of false appetite, or a fear of disease. Live in the realization:

Thank You, Father; I have no needs. You know my needs.

That is living by Grace. That is living by the Infinite Invisible, and you have moved out from under karmic law to Grace.

Every patient who comes to you is under karmic law, and in order to free him you realize in your treatment that he is no longer under the law but under Grace. No law of cause and effect is operating in divine Consciousness—only the law of divine Grace in which man does not live by bread alone, but by every word that proceeds out of the mouth of God. This you must do for your patients and students just as I do it for mine. You hold everyone in spiritual freedom by knowing that he is not under the law of karma—not as a result of former incarnations, present ones, or incarnations to come.

Mortal man has to earn his living by the sweat of his brow: spiritual man is joint-heir with Christ in God to all the heavenly riches. You are that spiritual man when the Spirit of God dwells in you, when you come to the place of acknowledging that you do not live under the law of cause and effect, that it is not *really* a law. It stems only from a belief in a selfhood apart from God, arising out of a false sense of self which permits itself to be brought under the law. If you believe that you, of your little self, are responsible for paying next month's rent, you have brought yourself under the law, but if you realize and acknowledge that you and the Father are one and that you do not live by bread alone, you have brought yourself under Grace.

Whenever you become a witness to some form of discord in a person, condition, circumstance, or place, be alert to realize that this is karmic law and that this law is not a power. "Neither circumcision availeth any thing, nor uncircumcision." [6] The new creature is subject not to what he does or does not do, but unto

[6] Galatians 5:6.

the grace of God. When you witness any form of error, what you must do is to release the victim from the law of karma, release him from the law of cause and effect, because it never was a law.

The son of God has power to forgive sins on earth, and you, in your divine sonship, can walk up and down this earth forgiving sins and healing sickness. It does not mean that all who touch your consciousness will respond to it because there are those who rigidly hold themselves under the law, and even if they were given their freedom, they would hasten back to their former state of bondage.

People can be given liberty, but no power on earth can make them keep it. The Hebrews had to go out and find a king to rule over them. Others have to join societies or unions; and some have to go out and find other kinds of associations for themselves because they cannot measure up to the responsibilities of freedom. Freedom cannot be given to everyone because everyone is not ready to accept it. But it can be given to everyone spiritually and silently, and those who are ready for it will respond to it. Those who are not ready for it will have to go on for a while, but it is not your concern what they do: your concern is what you do.

If you hold anyone in bondage to the law of karma, you have bound yourself. If you set him free, you have set yourself free because there is only one Self. What you do to another returns unto you; the bread that you cast upon the waters comes back to you. You suffer only because you are holding yourself under the law of cause and effect, but you can walk out on the waters of life in the realization that as the child of God you are no longer under the law, but under Grace.

Every time a discord comes into your experience, just smile at it, "Yes, that is still a part of the law, but I am under Grace, and that law is not a power. That law does not bind the child of God."

There is no karmic law except what men bind upon themselves by their acceptance of it. Should you teach your children that two times two equals five, I am sure you could get them to believe it and forever suffer from such a belief—suffer because they would have been brought up under that mistaken law or belief. The truth of this has been demonstrated in metaphysics for the past ninety years, but never has it been revealed in this particular way, a way that frees all men everywhere of everything, and releases them into their birthright of divine Consciousness, in which there are no human laws operating on them because they are a law unto themselves: "I am the way, the truth, and the life" [7]—*I* am the law. Until you are released into your true identity, there will be laws operating on you, but they will not be God's laws: they will be laws of man's creating.

Eliminating the Personal Sense of "I"

Man has made laws—religious, medical, legal, social, commercial, and governmental—and they have become binding upon you. But no one has a right to make laws for you, not even God. God is the law unto Himself and unto His own life, lived as you and as me.

Eventually this will lead you to what is undoubtedly one of the deepest revelations of The Infinite Way. The personal sense of "I" must be eliminated from your life, and in the degree you succeed in doing that will you know successful and joyous living. The word "I" must disappear entirely. You must be willing to give up the good as well as the evil sense of "I"; you must be willing to give up the rewards as well as the punishment.

This revelation has its source in the words of Christ Jesus who voiced it in these passages: "Why callest thou me good? there is none good but one, that is, God.[8] . . . The Son can do

[7] John 14:6.
[8] Matthew 19:17.

nothing of himself, but what he seeth the Father do.[9] . . . If I bear witness of myself, my witness is not true.[10] . . . I can of mine own self do nothing.[11] . . . My doctrine is not mine, but his that sent me." [12]

Many years ago I tried to teach our students the Middle Path, but resistance to it was very strong. It was at a time when everyone wanted to pray for peace, so I said to them, "Suppose you knew that Russia was going to drop an atomic bomb on us tonight, would you be in favor of our dropping one first, or would you let Russia go ahead and drop one before we did? Do not answer me now. Think it over until tomorrow."

The following morning the answer came from two mothers who showed me how impossible it was for them to accept such a teaching at that time: "I could do this for myself, but not for my children."

There can be no peace as long as there is war in the hearts of men, as long as the law of self-preservation is accepted. But if you can eliminate the word "I," neither you nor your children will have any life to lose. It is then God's life, and God can take care of His own. If you say, "God is my life," you must trust your life to God, not to the defensive power of an atomic bomb. You do not have to raise your hands in defense of your life, but neither can you feel that you are more righteous or more civilized than others. You must not take credit for the good that flows through you: whether it is healings or whether it is dedication to this message.

When I had been in the healing work for a short time and met one evening with a group of practitioner-friends, the subject of love came up. To me, this was a very strange subject. I could not understand love because I could not feel it. My friends said to me, "We look on you, Joel, as one of the most loving of persons.

[9] John 5:19.
[10] John 5:31.
[11] John 5:30.
[12] John 7:16.

You work so hard for your students and for your patients." I was unable to understand this either, because I certainly did not feel loving. I could not understand the words "love," "benevolent," and "spiritual." Certainly I did not feel spiritual and never have felt spiritual, but at least I now know the reason. It is because the personal "I" in me "died" when I had my first spiritual experience.

Certainly this little "I" is not loving or benevolent or spiritual. Whatever qualities may flow through me are flowing from the Source. There is nothing personal whatsoever about them. It is the Christ living individual life, Truth manifesting Itself and projecting Itself into human consciousness. We should be grateful that we can be instruments or avenues through which to show forth God's glory. As "the heavens declare the glory of God; and the firmament sheweth his handywork," [13] so much more are we the glory of God when the little "I" has been overcome. When the Master said, "I have overcome the world," [14] I believe he meant "I have overcome 'me.' " The "me" who can be rewarded and the "me" who can be punished—both have to go.

You cannot imagine how foolish the human scene seems when you are looking down from a spiritual height. For example, we are trying to arrive at an agreement with Russia not to drop an atomic bomb, and one of the greatest objections to such an agreement is that we are not sure we can trust Russia. Yet Russia has never dropped a bomb and we have—twice. We have not even said we are sorry that we did, nor have we said that we would not drop one again. So here we are worrying about the other fellow—and not looking in the mirror. This is the way the human scene looks because it is based on the law of self-preservation. But when "ten righteous men" begin to eliminate the personal sense of "I," they will know there is no karmic law and there is no law of cause and effect binding on the Christ, which is the *I* of their being and of yours and mine.

[13] Psalm 19:1.
[14] John 16:33.

As you now behold evidences of sin, disease, lack, death, and man's inhumanity to man—from the family circle to the international circle—quietly remind yourself: "In *My* kingdom, there is no karmic law; there is no law of cause and effect; there is no law of as-ye-sow-so-shall-ye-reap." As you do this, you will be nullifying the human belief that there is such a law, and just as some doctors are telling their patients that they can no longer catch cold by sitting in a draft or by getting their feet wet, so can we tell the world silently and secretly within ourselves: "There is no law of karma; there is no law of cause and effect; there is no law of as-ye-sow-so-shall-ye-reap. This is just as ancient a superstition as is the superstition that God is a God of rewards and punishments. It is not binding on spiritual man, and there is no other man."

Just as The Infinite Way has given to the world the restatement of the truth that God, Spirit, is the only power, so does it give to the world these two principles, which will release this world from the domination of a superstition it has come to accept as law. We have been prisoners of the mind for generations, and the mind has bound us with laws. But there is only one law, the law of God or Spirit. That law frees you and all who accept it from the domination of the mind.

At a certain stage of your unfoldment, you move out from being under the law to Grace. Then you must leave behind those things which have passed; you must forget the sins of your past and the errors of your old ways, and be a new creature under Grace.

In the twinkling of an eye, even though your sins were scarlet, you are white as snow. But do not carry your old selfhood around with you to remind yourself of the past. Today is a new day; today you are a new creature, born anew, born in Christ, spiritually and immaculately conceived, spiritually maintained and sustained.

THANKSGIVING MEDITATIONS

Meditations will vary in subject, in length, and in depth, depending on the occasion of the moment. Meditations must never be "formula-ized," nor must they ever follow a pattern, although in the course of a day or week certain specific points may recur for contemplation and meditation, not always in the same way, and not always will the meditations be of the same duration.

The following meditations are examples only of what has transpired in my consciousness and represent the contemplation of many facets of the spiritual life. Of course, by this, I mean my own spiritual life, since I cannot possibly know what has transpired in the consciousness of others who have lived the contemplative life.

As I sit in meditation, as the day dawns, I recognize:

This is Thy day, the day that Thou hast given us, and every moment of this day is filled with Thy Spirit, Thy grace, and Thy manna. I welcome this day with its labors, even its problems and its temptations, knowing that Thy Spirit fills every moment, knowing that Thy Spirit fills my consciousness, knowing that Thy Spirit fills my body. I welcome this day and every opportunity that it will bring me to show forth Thy glory, Thy presence, Thy grace, Thy manna.

Thy grace is my sufficiency in all things, in every department of my life. Thy grace is the substance of my day. Thou hast given me Thy manna, a daily manna, and I come to Thee now for my manna for today.

I cannot live by bread alone. I must have the Word that proceedeth out of the mouth of God. "Speak, Lord; for thy servant heareth." [15] *Let Thy word be revealed to me as manna for today, as wisdom to live the day, as guidance, protection, support, supply—just manna for today, Thy grace for this moment.*

Thou hast said, "Son, thou art ever with me, and all that I have is thine," [16] *and I come now to receive Thy grace, Thy manna for*

[15] I Samuel 3:9.
[16] Luke 15:31.

today, already established within me. I acknowledge that I can of my own self do nothing, that it is Thy Spirit that goes before me to make the crooked places straight and to prepare mansions for me.

It is Thy Spirit which is my strength; it is Thy Spirit which is my Grace, my meat, my wine, my water. Thy Spirit is my hidden manna, the meat I have that the world knows not of. I rest in Thy Spirit; I work in Thy Spirit; and I open my consciousness that Thy Spirit may flow to all those who touch my consciousness, that Thy Spirit may be loosed in the world.

As I partake of food three times a day, so do I also seek spiritual meat. Whether or not I eat the food that is set before me, in the morning, at noon, or at night, I cannot live without that food which is divine Grace.

I cannot live without Thy Spirit, Thy word. I listen to hear Thy word, to receive Thy word.

Renew me. Refresh me. Let me experience Thy manna for this moment. Let my meditations be acceptable in Thy sight, and let my consciousness be open and receptive to receive Thy grace. Thy grace is my sufficient manna unto this moment.

The evening is but a continuation of the day; it is a continuation of Thy grace.

Thou hast given us the light of day and the dark of night, both as a continuing spiritual Grace. Thou hast given us every moment of the day and every moment of the night, and filled each of these with Thy presence and Thy grace. This is my sufficient manna unto this moment, the manna that falls into my consciousness.

The word of God that is received in my consciousness is sufficient for my every need of the moment, whether it be a moment of work, a moment of rest, a moment of feasting or fasting, or a moment of play. Every moment of every day and of every night is filled with a sufficiency of Thy grace to meet every need, and always with those twelve baskets full left over to share with even "the least of these my brethren." [17]

As I go to my rest I remember:

This night will rapidly pass into day, with Thy grace continuing always throughout every moment, because I am receiving Thy manna when I sleep, as well as when I am awake. I am receiving

[17] Matthew 25:40.

Thy manna at rest, at work, or at play, for Thy grace is a continu-
ing experience, and there is this sufficiency of manna unto every
moment.

If, knowingly or unknowingly, human temptation has touched
me, nevertheless, I offer myself as I am, knowing that Thy grace
forgives and resurrects into newness of life, and Thy manna
nourishes that life. I cannot wait to be better than I am to offer
myself to Thee, and I need not be better than I am to receive for-
giveness, Grace, manna. It is now, here, just as I am, that I relax
in Thee and receive Thee: Thy word, Thy presence.

ACROSS THE DESK

Have you ever been faced with a problem and wondered how to
meet it? In that moment, then, you forgot that there was only
one power, and that your understanding of that made it unnecessary to meet anything. Have you ever been called upon to
meet some problem for someone and wondered if you had sufficient understanding, or if you had sufficient God-power? If so, in
that moment, you revealed that you did not know the truth.

It is not your knowledge of truth that meets problems or is
God-power: it is the realization that God is the only power. In
that realization, there are no problems to be met, there are no
laws to be overcome, there are no evils to be surmounted. All
these constitute the illusion of sense.

If you have been reading Infinite Way writings even for only
a short time, you must already know that God is, that this is
enough to know, and that since God is infinite, there can be
nothing besides God. Since God is omnipresence, there is no
other presence, no presence of evil or anything of a destructive
nature. Since God is omnipotence, there are no evil powers to
which to do anything, not even any evil thoughts. Since God is
omniscience, God is the all-knowing, and there is nothing else
for you to know, nor is there anything for you to do to anything,
or about anything, except to rest in the awareness of the is-ness
of God.

Do you think for a moment that by taking thought, even spiritual thought, you are going to change the harmony of God's kingdom, or that you are going to destroy a mythical kingdom?

As you sit in meditation, prayer, or treatment, do you realize that your only function is to abide in the *Is?* God is love: you are not going to make God love, or even make God loving. God is life: you are not going to save anyone's life or prevent anyone's death. You are to know the truth that makes free. Makes free of what? The ignorance and the superstition that believe in a power apart from God. But it is you who are believing in a power apart from God if you are reaching out to God for something or for someone.

Are your periods of prayer or treatment an abiding in the stillness, an abiding in the word that God is, or are you trying to do something to something? Are you trying to get God to do something to something, to someone, or for someone? Or are you abiding in *Is?*

God is, I am: this is enough to know. Are you still fearful for your patient, for your student, or for your child? Then treat yourself until you have risen to the awareness that regardless of all the evil appearances on earth, there is no more reality to these than to any illusion. Just as there is enough of God's grace and God's manna to meet the need of every moment, your knowing this truth removes you from any doubts or fears, and your patient or your student instantaneously responds to your awareness of God's *is-ness.*

God's grace is not dependent on anything, and this means that every student is sufficiently advanced to meet every need if he understands the principles of The Infinite Way, the principle of Is-ness and the principle of immediate Grace and the sufficiency of manna in every moment.

In every period of meditation, prayer, and treatment, relax all mental efforts, because your mental efforts can do nothing but frustrate you, and act as barriers to the realization of the instantaneity of spiritual peace, harmony, and wholeness.

Enter at once into stillness and quietness, listening for the still, small voice, because no amount of taking thought is going to be of benefit to anyone.

NOTE FROM HAWAII

SEPTEMBER 1963

In many classes I have touched upon mysticism in order to prepare our students for the unfoldment of the real meaning and function of The Infinite Way. Now, in the book, *A Parenthesis in Eternity,*[18] to be released November, 1963, my entire inner life is disclosed: my reason for living and my mission. The autobiography of my personal life would be boring: uneventful school days, routine business experience, and then out of the blue sky a spiritual experience. This book is my spiritual life as many of you have seen it from the outside, but here explained from the inside.

18 By the author (New York: Harper and Row, 1963).

TWELVE

The Revelation of Spiritual Sonship

———•———

One of the greatest lessons to be learned in the message of The Infinite Way has to do with the subject of prayer. It is only through prayer that our contact is established with the spiritual kingdom—the Kingdom that is within us, but to which we have no access in our human experience until we learn, in one way or another, how to bring it actively into our experience.

Very few persons today really question the existence of a God or of a spiritual realm, and I am sure that most persons who have given any thought to this subject must feel that there is a way to bring the power of this spiritual realm into what we call our human or daily experience.

Throughout all time people have been trying to reach that Kingdom. They have been trying to reach that Presence which they recognize as being beyond human power, beyond the range of human consciousness. All religions have had this as their goal, and that is the reason we have so many different forms of worship and prayer, and so many different religious beliefs.

Have not all these differences in religious teachings been brought about because of the failure of attempts to make contact with God and to bring His power into everyday life? Pagan religions failed in this attempt, and in the early centuries of the Judaic movement, only a few of the great spiritual leaders were able to make that contact and show it forth so that their followers could go and do likewise. But then the secret was lost. During the earliest days of Christianity, however, some spiritual lights did attain conscious union with this Presence and brought it forth on earth in active evidence. Then it was lost again, and because it was lost, we have had many centuries on earth without divine intervention.

Mankind Is on the Threshold of a Spiritual Age

We have already entered an age in which a reversal is taking place, and once again the secret of the mode and method of contacting God and the fruitage of it are being revealed. In the past century there has been definite evidence, not only that there are mental powers governing physical forces, but that there are spiritual powers that govern both mental and physical forces.

It is becoming more and more apparent, too, that the reaching out for this spiritual awareness is greater than it has ever been before, and that it is touching not only religious circles, but governmental, business, and industrial circles as well. All of this is indicative of the fact that we have entered a spiritual age in which more and more the nature of spiritual power is beginning to be understood and its demonstration on earth is being revealed.

The Christmas season gives us one of the best opportunities to witness the changes that are taking place in consciousness. There was a time in the early days of metaphysics when matter was denied. Then eventually it came to be realized that it is a fallacy to claim that there is no matter. Rather should we understand that matter is not what it seems to be.

Today we accept the truth of Paul's statement, "Know ye not that your body is the temple of the Holy Ghost?" [1] In other words, we no longer deny the body or that of which it is made, but rather realize that what the world originally believed to be a destructive and destructible thing called matter has now been proved, even scientifically, to be immortal and eternal.

So, too, the superstition and ignorance that once led to the acceptance of the Immaculate Conception and the Virgin Birth as a physical reality eventually were replaced by their denial. Yet, without these there can be no Christmas as an actual living experience on earth. Through enlightenment, we eventually come to see this whole idea in its proper perspective and to understand that immaculate conception and virgin birth are the only real truth about mankind—not merely about one individual, but about all men.

"Call no man your father upon the earth." [2] This statement should lead you to your first unfoldment on the nature of immaculate conception. True, in order to experience this you must rise above the level of the human mind and its tendency to judge by appearances. You must rise above what you see, hear, taste, touch, and smell into the intuitive realm, that realm in which you know, not by any human faculties, but by spiritual discernment, that is, by being receptive to what is revealed.

[1] I Corinthians 6:19.
[2] Matthew 23:9.

A New Concept of Prayer

This brings us to the subject of prayer, and why it is that in this age once again the nature of spiritual power on earth is about to be universally known and its availability demonstrated.

Most of the prayer of the world has been an attempt to enlighten God, tell, inform, or ask God, if necessary plead with Him, even bribe Him to do something or be something. Prayer has been an activity of the human mind. It has consisted of thoughts and words.

In the early days of our metaphysical and spiritual experience, we attempted to bring the presence and the power of God into the human scene, and in some way to manipulate it. Sometimes it was an attempt to bring the Spirit of God to the healing of the material concept of body, or to bring God to earth to stop wars or to save life in the midst of war. Sometimes we have even gone to God for supply.

The subject of supply best exemplifies the nature of the ignorance that fosters this attempt to use God. First of all, look out into the world and see if there is any lack of supply, any lack of trees, flowers, fruits, and vegetables, if there is any lack of gold, silver, platinum, oil, or minerals. Look out into this world and see if you can find a lack of any needful thing! Note rather the infinite abundance that has led some nations to destroy many of their assets. Think for a moment what it would mean to go to God and ask for more supply when already the earth is full of every good thing!

Now we are coming into an age in which it is beginning to be universally understood that prayer is not a human enlightening or influencing of God, but rather it is making ourselves subject to the divine power. The world is very rapidly learning to understand that prayer in its highest form is opening consciousness to receive light, wisdom, and understanding. It is the opening of consciousness that God's kingdom may be established on earth as it is in heaven, that God's will may be done with us, in us, and through us. This is the prayer that enables a person to admit humbly, "I can of my own self do nothing. Let Thy will be done in me and through me." There is now no longer an attempt to inform God of the world's needs; there is now only the opening of consciousness to receive the divine Grace that is already present within.

It is not as if God were a God afar off; it is not as if there were a God ignoring our needs. The kingdom of God, being within us, and the nature of God being omniscience, all-wisdom; omnipotence, all-power; omnipresence, all-presence, there is nothing for us to do in the realm of prayer except to listen. There is only the need to remember that God is not in the whirlwind; God is not in the outer scene: God is in the still small voice. The presence of God and the power of God are realized only in our ability to refrain from all attempts to inform or influence God and in proportion to our ability to hear the still small voice.

It does take a period of training until you can completely reverse the world's concept of prayer and bring yourself to a place where prayer is listening and receiving the activity of the divine Grace that is within, understanding that this can be done only in silence.

The Immaculate Conception

Once you attain the ability to listen and to receive this inner Grace, you are, in some degree, in possession of that mind which was also in Christ Jesus. It is at this point that you begin to receive instruction as to the nature of creation. When you do, you will find yourself in the midst of a real Christmas experience, and you will begin to understand the nature of the creation of man, and why it was that the Master was able to reveal God as the Father.

God is the Father! The first perception of that, be it ever so small, begins to change the nature of your life and the nature of your body. God is the Father; Spirit is the creative principle. This gives you your first light on the meaning of immaculate conception: God revealing, disclosing, and manifesting Himself as your and my individual being. This is conception completely separate and apart from physical processes. It is the divine creation, the creation revealed in the first chapter of Genesis in which man is made in the image and likeness of God, God individually formed, individually revealed, individually disclosed, the mind of God and the life of God manifest on earth as form. This is the immaculate conception and the virgin birth.

Our realization of the truth of immaculate conception may have been delayed because many of us have come to the mystical revelation of life through the mental sciences. In these mental sciences, we first rose above the belief that the body itself was all there is to us and that it had within itself the issues of life and death into a realization of the government of the body through the mind. This lifted us above the gross materialism of the early nineteenth century and the centuries prior to that, and enabled us to see that there is a realm beyond that of matter and form, an invisible realm, and yet a tangible one. Because that was the first step for many of us, we became accustomed to thinking of mind and thought as powers, not realizing that there was an *I* using both mind and thought, and that therefore there must be a realm beyond even that of mind.

That is where we are now. We have not discarded the body or matter or mind: we have merely relegated them to their rightful place as instruments of the *I* that I am, and subordinate to It. As we understand that *I,* we come to the Self of us which is immaculately conceived and of virgin birth. But this *I* never appears except as spiritual identity. That which we behold is only the mind and the body, but the *I,* the Self, the Reality is the God-

Self, the God-Being, the pure Being. This is what Christmas reveals.

Heretofore, it has been taught that there was only one son of God, one spiritually created individual; but in this age it is being revealed that the one Self which God is, you are, and I am. Now you begin to perceive God manifest as your individual being, and you begin to understand the immaculate and deathless nature of your being.

Christmas Reveals Immortal Indestructible Being

There is no way to experience immortality except through understanding that there is no beginning. Only that which is without beginning is without ending, and that is the identity that I am and you are. This is the Christmas revelation of the immortal being which we are.

Jesus did not claim for himself a different birth or a different creation, but spoke of "my Father, and your Father," [3] acknowledging that God was his Father and the Father of all, and therefore, all are one in divine sonship. He said, "I and my Father are one.[4] . . . Before Abraham was, I am" [5]—before the human sense of Abraham appeared on earth, *I AM,* and that *I AM* had its beginning in the beginning. *I* and the Father are indivisible, indivisibly one; and this means your Father and my Father. This is the Christmas revelation: "I and my Father are one.[6] . . . He that seeth me seeth him that sent me," [7] and this is the truth of your immaculate being, your spiritually conceived identity.

[3] John 20:17.
[4] John 10:30.
[5] John 8:58.
[6] John 10:30.
[7] John 12:45.

Once you understand that Christ Jesus did not claim a Selfhood separate and apart from yours or mine, you are living the Christmas experience, and you can discern the nature of the Christ-message, the revelation of spiritual sonship. Until you understand spiritual sonship, you can have no real Christmas, and for you Christmas will remain a pagan holiday. But when you realize the divinity of your being, the fatherhood of God and the spiritual nature of the Son, you have come into the Christmas experience; you have been awakened into the Christ-mass.

The secret is in the word *I:* "I am come that they might have life, and that they might have it more abundantly." [8] *I,* this divine Son, or Christ, which is your Selfhood, is the eternality and the perfection of your being. Without this *I* at the center of your being, without this divinity as the nature of your being, where is your immortality, where is your God-government?

Human Selfhood "Dies"
That the Christ May Be Born

So, as you abide more and more in silence and receive light from within, you discover that God has planted peace on earth: abundance, harmony, and health. By looking out through the five physical senses, however, you have not perceived the nature of this spiritual universe, and you have built a universe out of the second and third chapters of Genesis, a creation of your own in which you have placed labels on everything and named some things good and some things evil. But remember that as long as you persist in looking out through the human mind, you will continue to witness good and evil, abundance and lack, health and disease, life and death. It is only as you learn to be still and listen for the still small voice that the revelation is given to you of the spiritual nature of your being. The Christ-birth then takes place within you, and the human selfhood "dies."

[8] John 10:10.

The human selfhood cannot be spiritualized; the human self-hood cannot receive the grace of God because it does not know the things of God. To receive the things of God, it is necessary to "die daily." To look out into the world and acknowledge the infinite abundance that exists is really "dying" in a measure to the belief in abundance and lack because it is plainly evident that there is not abundance *and* lack: there is only abundance. What man has done to that abundance, however, is quite a different story, but the abundance is there, ready to spring into visible manifestation with a change of consciousness. Look out constantly into this world of abundance, and you will notice that part of you, that part of you which believed in lack, has "died."

So it is, as more and more of this mind that was in Christ Jesus becomes your mind through listening, through this higher experience of prayer, you are enabled to look out and discern that health and wholeness are the reality. Nowhere in God's kingdom is there an opposite, and it is only insofar as you are governed and molded by this belief in two powers that you experience what is called the human world, the world of good and evil.

You "die" to the belief of the human mind only as you are instructed by the still small Voice, as this Voice has an opportunity to reveal to you Its nature and Its presence, for It is the Comforter.

In a measure, you "die" to your humanhood through pondering the nature of your Father which is in heaven, your only Father, thereby enabling you to ponder the nature of your Self, that Self immaculately conceived and spiritually brought forth as the Christhood of your being, that in you which was never born and will never die, that which as heir of God does not live by might or by power, not even by pleading with God, but which lives by Grace. This is your divine sonship, your individual life that is lived by Grace, by virtue of your being an heir, not by the sweat of your brow.

Begin to realize that the reason for Christmas is the revelation of your Self, your divine sonship. The Spirit of God that was made manifest through Christ Jesus is proof for all time of the spiritual nature of your identity.

The Spiritual Interpretation of Givingness

The practice of giving gifts originated when the wise men and all those who had spiritual vision brought their offerings to the Christ-child. It is this same recognition today that impels those of spiritual vision to honor the spiritual teacher. Gifts are brought to that teacher, also. First they are brought in thanksgiving for the good that has been experienced in individual life, but later these gifts are brought for another reason, and that is as a recognition of the revelation of divine sonship.

To whomever you bring your gift, let it be as a recognition of his Christ-identity. Then offer your gift, not to your child, your parent, or your friend, but offer your gift to the Christ by recognizing the Christ-identity of those to whom you give gifts. Transform the commercial sense of Christmas even with its so-called material giving into a spiritual awareness of Christmas, so that every gift you give will be not of a materialistic nature, but an offering to the Christhood of the individual.

"Inasmuch as ye have done it unto one of the least of these my brethren, ye have done it unto me," [9] the Christ. Inasmuch as you have given your gift to the least of these, you have given it unto the Christ. Do you not see how you can transform the nature of your relationship to one another, and eventually the relationship of everyone in the world, through the recognition of this spiritual relationship?

[9] Matthew 25:40.

Peace on Earth

Peace on earth will not come through the seizing of power or the possession of power. Peace on earth eventually will come through the recognition of your spitirual identity, and mine. There is no other way.

Christmas is a revelation of your divine sonship, of the immaculate nature of your being since before Abraham was and unto the end of the world. But Christmas reveals the necessity of understanding the *universal* nature of spiritual being, the immaculate conception of all being, because of the fatherhood of God and the brotherhood of man.

This cannot come while we are thinking of ourselves as human beings of different races, religions, and nationalities. This can come only when we "call no man [our] father upon the earth: for one is [our] Father, which is in heaven." [10] That Father is not a Protestant, a Catholic, a Jew, a Vedantist, or a Buddhist. That Father is divine Being—just as you are neither Christian, Jew, or Buddhist, but rather the son of God, the Christ-being, God-Self revealed.

Christmas Message

Many, many times the Christ has appeared on earth as an individual: Lao-tze, Buddha, Shankara, Jesus, John, Paul, Nanak, and many others. Now the time has come when the Christ must appear as every individual. That is the activity, the function, the purpose, and the reason for the message of The Infinite Way.

The Infinite Way has been sent to prepare the consciousness of the world, not for the second coming of Christ, but for the

[10] Matthew 23:9.

first coming, since the Christ has never been on earth as universal consciousness, and The Infinite Way is preparing the world for the first experience of the Christ as the consciousness of mankind.

The message that has been given to me is that "the natural man," the man of earth, that man who receiveth not the things of God, is to be replaced by the man who has his being in Christ, the son of God. Throughout the 1961 and 1962 classes, the subject was "Raising Up the Son of God in You," lifting up the son of God in you. This does not mean a personal "you," but *you,* the consciousness of mankind.

Whatever The Infinite Way accomplishes with you as a person or with any of our teachers or practitioners is incidental only to the major function which is to reveal the first coming of the Christ *as the consciousness of mankind.* This will be the first time that this has ever happened on the face of the globe, and it will be the last time because the Christ will never be lost once it is established. The Christ can be lost when it comes as the consciousness of only one individual or even as the consciousness of one group because when that individual or that group leaves the earth the consciousness departs, but when the Christ comes as the consciousness of mankind, it will never again be absent from the world.

ACROSS THE DESK

A great deal of mail comes to my desk from people who write that they want "to work things out spiritually," and I am very frank in saying that I do not believe most of them. Many write of difficulties that involve financial or legal matters, but they say that they do not want to take legal steps: they claim that they want "to work it out spiritually." Actually, what they are doing is just trying to evade a normal, natural responsibility.

In every instance, where there are legal matters involved—in the matter of a will, real estate and brokerage deals, or royalty contracts with a publisher—I have them taken care of by obtaining the best legal advice I can find. Sentiment plays no part in that with me—only integrity, experience, and ability. If those to whom I turn for professional advice have those qualities, they can follow any religion they choose to follow.

We have no right to take anyone on faith simply because he is an Infinite Way student, a Christian Scientist, or a Unity student. Being affiliated with any of these, or for that matter with any religious group, does not necessarily mean that a person has attained the consciousness of that teaching. Even if students have attended Infinite Way classes, it does not mean that they have attained the degree of consciousness which will guarantee their right conduct. Because of human temptation, it is not easy for all of them to keep themselves immaculately clean in their dealings with others.

No one should choose a stockbroker, a real estate broker, or a lawyer because he is an Infinite Way student. If I were to choose any of these, I would choose him for his professional ability and integrity. I do not care if he is an Infinite Way student or an atheist. Ability and integrity, not religion, would be the determining factors in engaging his services. Of course, if there is a competent real estate broker or lawyer available and he happens to be an Infinite Way student, I might choose him, but never simply because he is in The Infinite Way.

Many persons may find fault with this way of thinking, but this is my way of doing business. I am telling you how I feel about such matters, not only for your own sake, but more especially so that you can tell others with whom you come in contact, because the longer you are in this work, the more persons are going to come to you for advice: advice on hotels, stockbrokers, lawyers, and bankers.

In any of your affairs, do not take things for granted and say, "Let God do it," thereby pursuing a policy of drift. Neither should you take a person's word in matters of business as if he were the final and ultimate authority. To do that is to rest on something as transient as the grass in the field, here today and gone tomorrow. Use your God-given intelligence on the highest level you can, but this, you have not done at all when you say, "I am going to leave it to God."

Now let us be clear about this: As spiritual students, we must never do anything without turning within, and then we should listen, never making a move or doing anything without inner guidance. Regardless of how informed and capable you are in any area, first turn within and seek that inner guidance.

Lead the contemplative life, but at the same time take every practical human footstep to let the Word become flesh. Sometimes things are brought right to your doorstep. On the other hand, there are times, as in the case of employment, when it is correct to go and seek for employment. That would be right activity. It is not that your good comes *from* those footsteps, but sometimes it comes *through* them.

In living the life of the contemplative, you will find that you are living a life attuned to an inner rhythm, an inner Grace. The more you listen and contemplate within, the greater protection and guidance you have on the outer plane.

The contemplative way of life is the most practical of all ways because it turns you within to the Source. You can lose anything on the outer plane—your home, business, or bank account—but if you have your contact within, with the only real Substance, eventually all losses will be turned to profit. As you practice this, it will not be long before you discover the wisdom of it.

Many persons write to tell how much happier they have been since studying The Infinite Way, even though their income has not increased. Perhaps they are not aware that doctor's bills are less, expenses for amusements have decreased, and money spent for practitioners is less because they have not had to call upon them so frequently. The income may not have vastly increased, but there are many places where money is not being spent. Money now fulfills a higher purpose because they are making contact with the only real substance there is: God.

Whatever spiritual inspiration you receive within, adapt it to your human experience. This inner life manifests itself above all things in human relationships and at every level of life. In your conduct and attitude toward the stranger or those closest to you, there must be the same integrity, the same tolerance, the same patience, and the same forgiveness. This does not in any sense mean that you permit yourself to be taken advantage of. Your inner wisdom would quickly remove any such conditions from you.

When you lead the contemplative life, you do not live for yourself only. Even if you go off to a cave, multitudes will find you, and through you they will find freedom. When you touch God, it does not mean that you will sit on Cloud Nine. In some measure, you will be called upon for your light so that others may also be set free.

As part of The Infinite Way student group, you have a responsibility. You will be called upon to share your light with others. God will not let you store up spiritual treasures for your own benefit. Of those who have much, much will be demanded, and the more treasures you lay up, the more often will you be called upon.

If you set yourself free from the world's problems, you have less of lack, sin, and disease, but the strange thing is that this freedom bestowed upon you is not for yourself alone. Soon someone comes to you for help, and, if you rise high enough, all the world will beat a path to your door. This, I have witnessed in my own experience and in that of students.

For example, when I touch the Kingdom within, do not think God says, "Oh, Joel, *I* heard you." No, it is released in consciousness. Whatever freedom I have gained has been shared with people around the world, and through whatever measure of freedom has been given our Infinite Way teachers, others also have found a degree of freedom.

The Master's whole teaching is a lesson in how to bring ourselves into at-one-ment with God. Nothing we can do humanly will influence God or add God's grace to us, but when we can come into obedience to God's laws, we can attune ourselves to spiritual law.

Through the contemplative life, we gain a much higher awareness of the meaning of equality; we see what the Master meant by one Father, and in our recognition of that, others will be set free.

There is a story of the angel of the Lord who came down and stood beside a man who had lived a long, long life of devotion to other people and said to him, "God wants to reward you for all your devotion to others. What would you like?"

His reply was, "What I would like most of all is that everyone who passes across my shadow be healed of all his problems, sins, and diseases, and that I never know who passed across that shadow."

And just as the woman who pressed through the throng and touched the hem of the Master's robe was healed, so many persons may be healed of sickness and sin by passing across our shadow, and yet we will have no awareness of a healing taking place or of our being "spiritual."

Many students want to feel that they have spiritual power or that they are blessing somebody, but that is only ego. Many persons, too, want to be "do-gooders" and help mankind, but when the little "I" gets in and makes them want to do something, it will not happen. The personal sense of "I" must be kept out of it. We cannot know when the Spirit functions. We are only witnesses, transparencies, panes of glass through which the sun shines.

In my thirty-two years of practice, I have never had a feeling that I have healed anyone. I only know it when someone tells me he has been healed. Personally, I had nothing to do with his healing. I meditate merely so that I can feel the inner Grace. This does not alter the fact that in any healing there must be an individual with an uplifted consciousness, because without a person with such a consciousness, the healing probably would not have taken place. That may seem like a contradiction, but nevertheless healing is always dependent on the degree of the illumined consciousness of an individual.

The Infinite Way teaching is based on God as individual consciousness. Without an illumined consciousness, the work will not be done. The works are done, not by you or by me as a wielder of power, but as a transparency through which the power can function.

The ego loses its sense of being a power when contact is made with the Life-stream. In proportion to your receptivity, you will benefit by your study, but that is also a matter of Grace. If you spend only ten minutes a day in study, that is probably because that is the limit of your capacity. But when that capacity expands, you will spend two hours or five hours. It is all dependent on an inner Grace.

Once you have learned the specific principles of The Infinite Way, let them drop out of your mind and sink into your heart, and you will draw on what you have stored up. Then, after you have meditated, do something completely different: go to a movie, watch television, or read some good book. When you are not consciously thinking of God, at the moment It is needed, It will come. Then, as you live normally, the divine Grace establishes Itself, and It speaks to you.

NOTES FROM HAWAII

OCTOBER 1963

It would be helpful for Infinite Way students to undertand the true meaning of the holidays of all religions, but at least they should know the esoteric meaning of the major holidays of the Christian faith. This is important because during these holidays we should know and practice the prayers and meditations which will attune us with the Consciousness out of which these holidays have evolved.

In *The Contemplative Life*,[11] there are two chapters helpful in gaining an insight into two of the most significant special days for those who follow the Christ-teaching.

The chapter on "The Spiritual Christmas" will enable the discerning to enter into the spirit of Christmas, which must be accomplished before they can attain the Easter of their lives, which is explained in "The Esoteric Meaning of the Easter Week." This chapter deals with the Easter holidays, and an understanding of it will change the nature of your entire experience and lead to marked advancement in prayer and meditation.

I would like to share with you one of the most fruitful spiritual principles that I have witnessed at work. With this, I suggest that not less than twice, and if possible three times a day, you retire for a few moments to meditate on this principle. Be sure, however, that you are not merely repeating this idea with your mind, using it as an affirmation, or going through the motions of reading it. You really must know the principle that I am revealing to you.

> *God's grace is my sufficiency in all things. God has given me a sufficiency with which to meet my every moment's need. Just as I receive only enough air in my lungs for this second's breath, and then a second from now I receive enough air for that second, so every second of my life I receive from the Father within sufficient Grace unto that moment and unto the fulfillment of every requirement of every moment.*
>
> *Since God does not operate in the past, there is no way for God to give me anything in the past. Since God cannot possibly operate in the future, God cannot give me anything at all in the future; and therefore, the activity of the grace of God is at work in my consciousness now to provide for this particular moment, and to provide abundantly with twelve baskets full left over to share.*
>
> *As I remember the barren trees of the winter, it is brought clearly to my mind that God's grace is functioning in those trees to fulfill every requirement of every moment so that eventually in the spring and summer of their fulfillment, the day comes when*

[11] By the author (New York: The Julian Press, 1963).

the leaves and the buds, the blossoms and fruit appear outwardly.
But if God's grace had not been operating throughout the winter
to provide for every second's need, the fulfillment could not have
appeared in the spring and summer.

So, too, regardless of any outer appearances, I understand now
that God's grace is a sufficiency unto every experience of this moment's life and unfoldment. If I look back into the past, I see the
penalty of my own belief in the absence of God in all the negative
experiences that have happened to me. If I look forward into the
future with anxiety, concern, or fear, I dishonor God and show
my ignorance of how God operates because now I have learned
that God can operate only in the now, and that whatever of God
is being expressed can be expressed only in the now.

If I look at the sunshine, I realize that the sun can shine only
each second at a time, and each second it is fulfilling its function
as the sun. Even as I look at the clock it is ticking only this second. Even a clock cannot operate in the future.

Since I realize now that God's grace is functioning universally
in the consciousness of every individual, I realize further that
God's grace is functioning in this second to fulfill every require-
ment, every need, every joy of this moment. I now begin a new
pattern of living in this moment, and of living each second at a
time, knowing that in this second God's grace is at work in the
consciousness of every individual in every part of the globe.